RULES FOR FREEDOM OF FAITH

Defining Religious Liberty for a Harmonious World

AN RAN

Rules for Freedom of Faith: Defining Religious Liberty for a Harmonious World

Cover design: Tingjun Lin

ISBN: 978-1-967799-81-7
Library of Congress Control Number: 2025928020

Published and distributed in January 2026 in the United States by
Asian Culture Press LLC
1942 Broadway St., Suite 314c
Boulder, CO 80302
United States

Printed in the United States of America

Preface

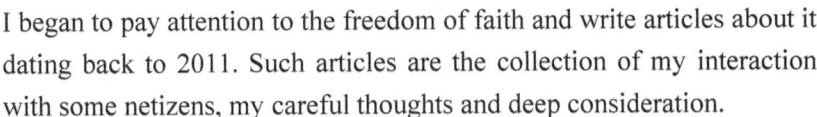

I began to pay attention to the freedom of faith and write articles about it dating back to 2011. Such articles are the collection of my interaction with some netizens, my careful thoughts and deep consideration.

If I were to recommend this book myself, I would say that the world lacked a regular understanding about freedom of faith. Instead, all religions, including the normal religion and forced religion, were mixed up. In the absence of rules for freedom of faith, it seems that autocratic systems are more likely to outlaw some normal religions at will, while democratic systems seem to be more tolerant of forced religious faith. Therefore, normal religion seems to be more likely to be suppressed, while forced religious faith seemingly remains to be sheltered.

Built on a case-by-case, reasonable, and well-founded basis to the greatest extent, this book is written precisely for the above purpose. Because the normal religion and forced religion can be understood and treated distinctly only when the relevant logic and facts are clarified with the correct rules, thereby facilitating the reform on the relevant forced religion. As the reforms aim to eliminate the practice taken by forced religion, such a religion can turn into a normal religious faith that everyone can choose freely.

Contents

Chapter 1 Rules for Freedom of Faith

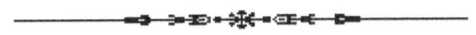

Various things in the world are easy to be hypercorrect. For example, goodness is positive, but it would be wrong if the goodness is used to tolerate the evil. By the same token, it would be good to grant freedom of faith to the normal religions, but it would be wrong to grant freedom of faith to some religious practices that contain forced faith, because this is actually tantamount to anti-freedom of faith. Thus, it can be seen that the meaning of freedom of faith cannot be defined by personal likes and dislikes, but should be defined according to the correct rules.

I.   Current profile of freedom of faith in the world:

1.   In some autocratic countries, normal religions are suppressed or even persecuted.

2.   Religious laws exist in many countries, such as some Islamic countries in the Middle East, and believers are not allowed to have the right to withdraw from and convert their faith freely.

3.   Although democratic countries such as Europe and the United States advocate freedom of faith, their understanding about it is still partial, where the attention is only paid to the freedom of believing in and praising a religion, but there is a lack of understanding of the freedom of despising and not believing in a religion. In addition, in these countries, the implementation of religious laws, and some religious practices, such as the absence of freedom of withdrawing from faith, existing in some local regions, are often ignored and tolerated.

From the above three points, we can see that there are severe problems about the understanding of freedom of faith in the whole world, and thereby it is particularly important to clarify the relevant rules for freedom of faith.

II.   We should recognize the difference between normal religion and forced religion:

1.   Religion can be divided into normal religion and forced religion. Normal religions can only be defined as individual religious beliefs, where believers can only demand themselves personally with religious teachings, but cannot demand others with their religious teachings, which is the most fundamental difference between normal religions and forced religions.

2.   Normal religion must allow anyone to freely choose the right to believe it or not, and to freely choose to praise or belittle it words.

3.   Normal religions endow believers with the right to accept anyone's free choice to believe it or not, and to praise or belittle them it freely in words. The government and the people should respect this right and legitimacy of the existence of this religion. Any country or nation should have such a broad mind and understanding about religions.

4.   Forced religious faith allows believers to demand others with religious teachings. In other words, religious teachings are not just used to demand believers themselves only.

5.   Forced religious faith may have the following characteristics: (1) Freedom of religious expression is not allowed, that is, the right to criticize and belittle the religion does not exist. (2) Believers tend to demand and compel each other with religious teachings, and even put forward coercive demands to non-believers and society, depriving of the characteristics of individual religious belief. (3) Believers are not allowed to have the right to withdraw from and convert their faith freely.

III.   We can hereby clarify the correct rules for freedom of faith:

1.   Freedom of faith includes the right for anyone to choose to believe it or not, and to choose to praise or belittle any religion in words. The country should provide legal protection to citizens' right to freedom of faith and freedom of religious expression.

2.   For any normal religion that recognizes and supports this freedom of faith, the country should respect and recognize the right and legitimacy existing in this religion, and endow relevant legal protection.

3.   For any religion that opposes this freedom of faith, such as the lack of freedom of choosing to believe it or not, withdraw from the religion, and to freely praise and belittle the religion, the country should impose legal restrictions on such the religion and urge its reform.

4.   The final dogma shown by any religion shall not breach the normal national law. Otherwise, the country has the right to restrict and amend the implemented doctrine that violates the law.

5.   Neither does the government have the right to casually judge whether a religion is an "orthodox religion" or a "cult", "orthodox" or "extreme", nor does it have the right to judge the doctrine of any religion on the basis of some people's subjective likes and dislikes, so as to divorce religion from government. The country has the right to restrict and amend its relevant teachings in accordance with law, only when the religion actually violates the above-mentioned rules for freedom of faith, or violates the normal laws of the state regarding its implementation of doctrine.

Chapter 2 Freedom of Religious Expression

Note: nowadays, many people's understanding about freedom of faith is only limited to the idea that they have the freedom of faith and praise, but they do not realize that freedom of faith also includes freedom of non-faith and belittling. Thus, I hope that the freedom of religious expression described in this article can establish a consensus for all, and inform everyone of a basic rule for freedom of religious expression, so as to alleviate the contradictions between different religious believers and help them coexist peacefully.

1. True Meaning of Freedom of Faith

The so-called freedom of faith refers to the freedom of praising a religious faith in words, and the freedom of belittling it, which also includes the freedom of arguing with each other on the premise of mutual respect.

For the general public, faith can be said to be a part of thought, which naturally allows people to tolerate other thoughts. Whether people praise or belittle a kind of faith, such the faith should be given freedom of expression. For example, if someone belittles a kind of religious faith, then people who believe in that religious faith should not be dissatisfied with this guy or hate him, because if they believe in the faith, they should give each other freedom of thought and speech. Therefore, if a person belittles a religious faith, then his view is still part of his freedom of expression or belief, which is essentially different from the action of belittling a specific person, group or race in real life.

For the specific faith for individuals, faith can be said to be equal to truth. In essence, believers must not be afraid of being questioned and verbally opposed by others, because faith is tantamount to truth, and truth fears no attack and opposition. If a faith fails to accept or dreads to accept the questioning and opposition from other people, then it shows that the so-called faith is narrow, which also indicates that it is not a true or correct faith in itself, and it is definitely not the same as the truth. This is also the characteristic of truth as said by Galileo: "The truth is to have such power: the more you want to attack it, the more enrich and prove it." Therefore, if it is a true or correct faith, it is equal to the truth, and it will certainly allow others to freely evaluate it in words without the narrow-minded sense.

Therefore, if someone today is dissatisfied with or hates a person because this person belittles his or her faith, it shows that he or she has developed a kind of narrowness in his or her faith, and there have been even restrictions on the freedom of thought and speech of others. However, if the belittled views about other people can be corrected on the premise of mutual respect, or ignored due to the respect for freedom of speech, such practices are all undoubtedly appropriate.

Therefore, we can say that religious faith falls into the category of public thought, which is different from specific people and things, and the public is allowed to exchange and discuss their views in words, to choose whether to believe it or not, and to praise or belittle it. As said by Voltaire: "I disapprove of what you say, but I will defend to the death your right to say it." That's why we all may have different religious faiths, but each other must defend to the death the right and freedom of others to express different views on each religious faith, even if their views are about belittling a faith. If everyone of different religious faiths can tolerate and respect other people's different views, then the world will be pluralistic and harmonious. Furthermore, the faith will also be revealed as the true faith, proving to be the truth.

2. Everyone Should Respect the Freedom and Right of Others to Belittle A Religious Faith

We are aware of the fact that the teachings and objects of different religious faiths are different, explaining why they naturally repel each other and cannot be reconciled at all. For example, if a person believes in Islam, he or she will certainly think that Christianity is wrong. If a person believes in Christianity, he or she will also certainly think that Buddhism is wrong. Therefore, we must all admit that it is an objective fact that different religious faiths are mutually exclusive. In response to this phenomenon, we have to ask, since the teachings of different religious faiths are different and mutually exclusive, can people of different religious faiths coexist peacefully? The answer is yes, because although different religious faiths cannot be reconciled, people of different religious faiths can coexist peacefully.

First of all, we must make a clear distinction: people with religious faiths and religious faiths are two different concepts. Religious faith falls into the category of public thought, not belonging to any individual or group. Instead, the religious faith represents the free choice that everyone voluntarily accepts or is unwilling to accept. Therefore, when a person belittles a certain religious faith, he or she is not belittling a certain person or group but is expressing his or her personal views on a certain religious faith. This is his or her own freedom and right. People of that religious faith should not only respect him or her, but also defend his or her freedom and right to express his or her views. This kind of respect and defense is the same as what Chinese ancients said: "gentlemen seek harmony but not uniformity".

But if someone claims that a religious faith is not allowed to be belittled by others, then we should say, for a religious faith that can only be praised but not belittled, then its praise and belief are meaningless, and such religious faiths are already compulsive.

We can also take advantage of the following facts to explain that everyone has the right and freedom to belittle any religious faith. The fact is that everyone has belittled a certain religious faith, and no one can be an exception. For example, when you believe in Islam, you are actually disbelieving and denying Christianity, indicating that you are already belittling Christianity; when you believe in Christianity or Buddhism, you are also belittling other religions; and when you do not believe in any religion, it actually stands for a certain disparagement against many religious faiths. Thus, since everyone has belittled the certain religious faiths, then who has the right to be dissatisfied with or hate others who belittle a religious faith?

Therefore, we are sure that we should respect everyone, but we do not need to respect a certain religious faith; we should respect everyone's will and right to believe in a religious faith, but we do not need to respect a religious faith. In other words, everyone must be respected, but respecting religious faiths is not necessary.

Thus, if we are to eliminate the divisions and misunderstandings between people of different religions in the world in order to achieve peaceful coexistence, we must all recognize the needs and rules for freedom of religious faith. This rule is: "everyone has the right and freedom to praise and belittle any religious faith." Nothing can be accomplished without rules. If there are no rules regarding the peaceful coexistence among people of different religious, then our efforts can only cure the symptoms, not the disease, even if we have many good wishes and take unremitting efforts.

3. Can I Express Protest Against and Dissatisfaction With Others Who Belittle A Religious Faith?

As someone has said, many contradictions in this world are not actually contradictions on views, but are often caused by differences in understanding due to the lack of a clear definition of the meaning of some nouns. Therefore, for some understanding about freedom of religious expression, it is necessary to clarify the differences between the following nouns, so as to explain what the boundary of freedom of religious expression is.

1.   Difference between criticism and protest

Criticism is different from protest, because criticism is a kind of correction, while protest is a negative opinion against the other party. For a religious faith, namely public thought, all people can express their views, including praise and belittling, and can communicate and discuss with each other and even criticize and correct each other on a case-by-case basis. However, having interfered with other people's right to freedom of belief, the protest is a practice of expressing negative opinion or hatred, where the forced scope of faith is involved.

2.   Can I express dissatisfaction with others who belittle a religious faith?

Of course not. For example, if a person praises Jesus, he or she benefits from Jesus; if the person belittles Jesus, he or she receives losses from Jesus. Here, whether he praises or belittles Jesus, the benefits and losses are his own business. What does he have to do with others? How can others be dissatisfied? This is true of Jesus, and the same is true of Mohamed. It can be seen that any dissatisfaction here is a sign of narrow mind.

3.   Take Christianity as an example

For a religious faith, some may praise it, and some may belittle it. To put it simply, if a person raises a sign on the street saying, "Jesus is a liar", will Christian believers have negative opinions or hatred against this person? Or you can adopt an objective attitude, as Voltaire said: "I disapprove of what you say, but I will defend to the death your right to say it." In fact, the above two different attitudes can be used to distinguish the nature of their treatment of religious faiths.

4.   Take Islam as an example

For a religious faith, some may praise it, and some may belittle it. Similarly, if a person holds up a sign on the street saying, "Hamad is a liar", will the followers of Islam have negative opinions or hatred against this person? Or you can adopt an objective attitude, as Voltaire said: "I disapprove of what you say, but I will defend to the death your right to say it." In fact, the above two different attitudes can be used to distinguish the nature of their treatment of religious faiths.

5.   Conclusion

In summary, believers of different religions, whether Christianity or Islam, can communicate and discuss with each other on different views, including praise and belittling, if someone belittles their religious faiths. They can also criticize and correct each other on different views, but none of them have the right to have negative opinions against and hate each other just because of their different views, such as protest, swearing, etc. Instead, they should respect each other's right to express their views.

4. What Is the True Freedom of Religious Expression?

If you ask what the true freedom of religious expression is, I believe many people's first response to this question is that this question looks too simple. But in fact, judging from the speeches by some people posted on the Internet, many people are not very clear about this question.

As can be observed on the Internet, when almost everyone talks about freedom of religious speech, apart from mentioning the freedom to praise religion, people only use some neutral words such as "criticism" and "comment" regarding the negative evaluation of religion, but they never dare to use such a direct negative word as "belittling".

But in fact, the antonym of "praise" is exactly "belittling", not just some neutral words such as "criticism" and "comment". In other words, in terms of the freedom of religious speech, since some people can use extremely positive words, such as praise and other words, then under equal rights, some people can also use extremely negative words, such as "belittle" and others.

Then why everyone is used to using words such as "criticism" and "comment", but never using words like "belittling"? This is because the meaning of "criticism" and "comment", according to the current context, is only limited to the well-intentioned criticism and reasonable criticism of religion, instead of malicious criticism. The meaning of "belittling" means that you can judge a religion at any time based on how you feel about a religion, or you can evaluate a religion anytime, anywhere, in good faith or maliciously. This is an individual's right to freedom of expression. Therefore, it can be seen that "criticism" and "belittling" are not words on the same level.

Therefore, it can also be seen that when your understanding about religious freedom of expression or negative evaluation of religion is limited to using neutral words such as "criticism" and "comment", it is actually just the same old story, without any new idea or value. Because the evaluation of this neutral word means that when you make a negative evaluation of a religion, it's fine if it makes people think it's a well-intentioned criticism, but if it makes people think it's not very mild criticism, then it can be interpreted as malicious criticism at any time. As a result, you may face considerable pressure in some places, or may even be charged with blasphemy in some parts of the world.

Thus, I would like to ask, if the negative evaluation of religion is limited to the use of words such as "criticism" and "comment", can it represent the true freedom of religious expression? Of course not.

What is the true freedom of religious expression anyway? The answer is that the religion is a kind of public thought, and some people can praise it, while others can not only criticize it, but also belittle it. This is the equal right to freedom of speech, and this is the true freedom of religious expression. The reduction of any of these rights constitutes the weakening and infringement of religious freedom of expression.

Speaking of which, I recall a story told in the famous Christian pamphlet "*Know the Truth*", which can be used to elaborate on this problem.

The story goes something like this. More than 100 years ago, there was an old man who died in North Minton, Ohio, at the age of 82. Before his death, he extremely attacked the Bible, saying that the Bible was fake. Prior to his death, he even built a tomb for himself. A monument was built on the tomb, and a bronze statue was carved for himself. The bronze statue held a piece of paper in his hand, saying "Men act at will." There is a book under the left foot, which represents the Bible. He exalted that man could do whatever he wanted and trample on the Bible. Before he died, he said, "if there is a God, or the Bible is true, may my tomb be inhabited by snakes." As a result, his graveyard is really inhabited by many snakes and is thereby locally known as the snake tomb.

We will not comment on the actual situation of this story, but we can see from this story, at least in the eyes of Christianity believers, no matter how the old man attacked and belittled the Bible during his life, and he even set up a bronze statue to step on the Bible after death, these all stand for the freedom of expression, although such words are mean. This kind of freedom of expression is widely accepted, as it is written in a quite well-known Christian pamphlet.

Therefore, from this story, we can also see what the true freedom of religious expression is, which is not only about the freedom of praise, but also about the freedom of criticism and comment, and the freedom of belittling a religion out of personal feelings anytime and anywhere. Any reduction on such rights will undermine the true freedom of religious expression.

5. The Freedom of Belittling the Religion Has a Positive Impact on It

━━━━━━━━ ━❖━ ━━━━━━━━

After I have proposed that everyone has the freedom to praise and belittle any religion, some religious believers may worry that if there is the freedom to belittle a religion, it will do harm to all religions. And I believe it is precisely out of this reason that many people in the religious circle failed to advocate the freedom of belittling the religion in the past.

However, this worry is unnecessary, because on the contrary, the freedom of belittling the religion is not only harmless to the religion itself, but also has a positive impact on all normal religions.

Before discussing this issue, I would like to clarify one concept again. That is, although everyone has the freedom to criticize and belittle any religion, he does not have the freedom to oppose other people's right to believe in the religion. This means that although you are free to belittle a religion and say how bad it is, you must also respect everyone's right to profess and praise that religion, which is a well-deserved boundary in the relevant rules on freedom of faith. With this in mind, let's start to talk about the freedom of belittling the religion and its positive impact on the religion.

1. The freedom of belittling the religion help normal religions achieve a balance of faith

There used to be a saying that if you are not free to criticize, then praise is meaningless. By the same token, since a normal religion, as a kind of public thought, has been praised by many believers, then under the same equal rights, the public (especially those who do not believe in the religion) should be allowed to have the freedom to belittle the religion, thus creating a balance of the religion in public speech.

What is the effect of this balance? On the one hand, religious believers have the right to the freedom of expression of praising the religion. On the other hand, from a public point of view, everyone also has the right to the freedom of expression of belittling the religion. This makes the public actually plays a role of cultural supervision of public opinion over the religion (here, we refer to the non-religious places of course.), preventing the public opinion from becoming excessively bigoted and irrational, and helping the normal religions achieve a balanced state.

Under the balanced public culture and public opinion, the devout religious followers will be more out of their free and smooth choice of personal will, rather than moving towards another excessive paranoid pursuit, so that they themselves get a balance of their own beliefs.

2.　　The freedom of belittling the religion to enable the normal religions to develop towards the positive direction

When the freedom of belittling religion becomes the consensus among the world, the various religions will naturally produce the phenomenon of survival of the fittest to a certain extent. At this point, some inferior religions either change themselves, take the essence and discard the dregs, get rid of related shortcomings and corrupt customs, and carry out self-improvement, or they will eventually be eliminated because they can't stand the revelation of the truth. But think about this: if a religion really cannot stand the public opinion because of its own problems, and refuses to improve and change, then it is no pity that it should be eliminated.

For those religions whose overall religious content is relatively reasonable or have been corrected and promoted, their believers not only get a more appropriate pursuit of religious belief, but also make the religion more attractive to the outside world, thereby making it easier for the religion to develop towards a positive direction.

3.　　The freedom of belittling the religion will only adversely affect the forced religion and promote its reform.

As I said earlier, the religion is divided into normal religion and forced religion. The freedom of belittling the religion will have the following different effects on these two religions:

For the normal religions, because there is no forced belief practice, when others belittle the normal religions, their followers will not have negative opinions and interference with others. Therefore, no matter whether people are aware of the freedom of belittling the religion or not, for all normal religions, this derogatory right has always been allowed to exist. Thus, even when people are universally aware of the right of the freedom of belittling the religion, it will not have any adverse effect on these normal religions.

On the other hand, it is a different story for the forced religion, because there are already some practices of forced belief, when people are not aware of the freedom of belittling the religion, people will have no way to belittle the religion. Otherwise, it will result in negative opinions and interference from its followers. However, when people generally recognize the right of freedom of belittling the religion, then for the forced religion, its right of not allowing people to belittle the religion must be changed, thereby promoting its own reform.

4. If there is no freedom of belittling the religion, it will eliminate the religion in turn

This truth is actually very simple. If there is no freedom of belittling the religion, then people will only dare to belittle the normal religion, but will not dare to belittle the forced religion. In this way, it will eliminate the religion in terms of religious expression in the first place.

Moreover, without the freedom of belittling the religion, believers of the forced religion will not be able to achieve a balance of beliefs, but will easily fall into some kind of paranoia, which may cause their believers to follow their teachings to demand others and even society as a whole, resulting in some kind of eliminating effect in the development of different religions in turn.

As a result, the normal religion may decline instead, while the forced religion may develop.

5.   The freedom of belittling the religion will also have a positive effect on the cultural form of the whole society

In fact, religion is also a kind of culture. It can be said that if the religion is the core, then culture is an extension of religion. Therefore, the so-called freedom of religious speech is actually a part of freedom of cultural speech. Therefore, when people can universally realize that the freedom of belittling the religion, it will have the same positive effect on the freedom of cultural speech of the whole society, and make the freedom of speech of the whole society more lenient. Therefore, it will have a positive impact on the cultural form of the whole society.

Chapter 3 Advocate the Separation of Islam from Politics, and the Separation of Nationality From Religion

Judging from the status quo of freedom of faith in the world today, especially in some Islamic countries, there is indeed a quite common phenomenon of the combination of politics and religion, and the bundling of ethnics and religion. Therefore, this chapter focuses on such problems existing in Islam today, and explains the relevant rules on freedom of faith.

1. On the Problem of the Integration of Politics and Religion in Some Islamic Countries

Today, the definition of "the integration of politics and religion" generally refers to a system in which political power and religious power are combined into one. However, such a definition is actually rather one-sided, because according to some actual phenomena in the world today, the integration of politics and religion is actually reflected not only in the system, but also in all aspects of a society. In addition, the superficial system is only one aspect of it.

How should the "integration of politics and religion" be fully defined? In a nutshell, as long as the laws of a country tolerate the religious teachings, support the practice of demanding people with the religious teachings, and impose relevant personal punishment on people, then it is actually a practice of the integration of politics and religion. If this practice is also universal to a certain extent, then the country can be regarded as a de facto country where the politics and religion are integrated.

At present, this kind of integration of politics and religion exists in many Islamic countries in the world. Thus, I will discuss the problem of the integration of politics and religion in these countries and explain the relevant rules on freedom of belief.

1.   The problem of the integration of politics and religion in some Islamic countries

In some Islamic countries, there is often a lot of confusion between the teachings of Islam and national laws. In these countries, their people can be required to abide by the teachings of Islam, but this is actually a combination of politics and religion. With regard to the irrationality of the integration of politics and religion, we can imagine that if its citizens (or some citizens, the same below) are required to believe in Islam and abide by the teachings of Islam in a country, that is to say, citizens in my country, namely China, should also be required to believe in and abide by the relevant rules of Confucianism, and citizens in India are required to profess a religion and abide by its dogma. Of course, this is absurd, because it is tantamount to depriving the citizens of a country of their right to freedom of faith.

2.   The essence of the integration of politics and religion is the forced belief

The so-called integration of politics and religion means that citizens of a country are required to believe in and abide by certain religious teachings, or that nationals of a country are required to choose only one religion and doctrine, which is actually a practice of forced belief.

3.   The integration of politics and religion is harmful to the religion itself

On the surface, the integration of politics and religion, which is actually the force belief, seems good for the development of a religion, but in reality, it is not. Because first of all, no matter whether a religious doctrine itself is good or bad, even if a religion with good teachings in itself is allowed to be praised by the public but not belittled within the scope of the integration of politics and religion, that is, it does not give the public the right to discuss freely, then even the best religion will certainly be monopolized by some people to exercise doctrinal monopoly, and the national law will be employed as the support to carry out doctrinal demands on the people. Such a religion is likely to move towards forced belief in doctrine because it is controlled by some people, and thus have a harmful effect on the religion itself.

4.   The harmful effect of the integration of politics and religion on the race and family

The integration of politics and religion will also lead to the forced belief in the whole nation and individual families and deprive all people of the right to understand and choose freely regarding different religions and doctrines. It is also easy to demand and compel those who know different religions among their race and individual families, thus making the whole nation and family fall into a negative environment of forced belief and faith. In other words, the integration of politics and religion in a country can easily be brought into its nation and individual families to produce some kind of binding and harmful effects.

5.   The harmful effects of the integration of politics and religion on the individuals believing in the religion

The integration of politics and religion in a country is not only disadvantageous to those who do not believe in its religion, but also has a harmful effect on those who believe in its religion. Because professing a religion should be a free and smooth choice for a person, if a person can freely choose a religious belief environment, then he can profess a religion according to his own wishes, without being affected by the compulsive environment such as the integration of politics and religion. However, if a person believes in a religion in an environment where the politics and religion are integrated, he will be easily influenced by the compulsive environment in which a part of people monopolize the discourse of doctrine. In this compulsive environment, he is also more likely to have some kind of religious paranoia, and even face extreme influence, thereby exerting a harmful impact on the personal religious faith.

Therefore, it can be seen that on the surface, the integration of politics and religion seems to be a kind of support for its believers, but in fact it will have a harmful impact on individual believers.

6.   The necessity for the separation between the politics and religion

It can be seen from the above that the integration of politics and religion will have a harmful impact not only on a religion itself, but also on its nation, family and individual believers. As a result, the whole country is in a social state of mutual demand for the integration of politics and religion. Therefore, if a country wants to have a normal social state, the separation of politics and religion is indeed necessary.

7. The basic principles of the separation between politics and religion

Here we need to clearly clarify and define the separation between politics and religion in order to understand where the boundary between a religion and national laws should be in a normal society, reflected in the following three basic principles of freedom of faith:

(1) As long as a religious group does not violate the national law, it has the right and legitimacy to exist.

First of all, for a religious group, as long as it does not violate the laws of that country, it falls into the normal scope of freedom of religious faith, and neither the government nor others have the right to interfere. Instead, the right and legitimacy of its existence should be respected. A country or race should have such a broad mind and understanding.

(2) Everyone has the freedom to choose whether or not to profess a certain religion or to abide by a certain religious doctrine.

Moreover, for a specific individual, as long as he has not violated the national law in his conduct, it is his personal freedom whether he is willing to profess a certain religion or to abide by a certain religious doctrine, no matter what kind of person he is. Here, no matter whether he is a Christian, Islamic or any kind of person, he should only represent an independent free individual.

(3) Each person's right to choose a religion is affected by his own individual freedom, rather than his own background.

Recently I read an article about Islam, which claims that the separation of politics and religion is truly realized, if the law of a country only requires Muslims (that is, Islamists, the same below) to abide by the rules of Islam, but not requires non-Muslims to abide by the rules. But of course, this statement is wrong, because every Muslim is essentially an independent individual of a national, and it is naturally included in the principle of separation of politics and religion in that country, as long as he does not violate the laws of that country, then it should be his personal freedom and right to abide by the rules of Islam and even to choose other religious faiths.

8. Conclusion

To sum up, it can be seen that some Islamic countries and their citizens have been adversely affected by the integration of politics and religion, and Islam itself is also affected by the integration of politics and religion because the discourse power of its teachings is easily monopolized. Therefore, these countries should begin to establish a normal system of separation of politics and religion, loosen the ties between the country and Islam, and restore the national law into the normal law and religion into the normal religion. Only by establishing such a separation system, can the citizens of these countries begin to have a normal environment of freedom of religious faith, and therefore have a normal social state under the sole authority of the national law, thereby eliminating the practice of governing people with the teachings.

2. Islamists Should be Unbound From the Name of "Muslim"

What does "Muslim" mean? Generally speaking, "Muslim" generally refers to Islam, but it may actually include a lot of content. According to the relevant information, "Muslim" can also refer to the entire Muslim world, and it can also refer to some Islamic countries in particular. In addition, some people think that "Muslim" refers to a certain ethnic group. In short, the name "Muslim" seems to include Islamists, some countries, and a conceptual ethnic group. Therefore, as many people may feel confused about the name "Muslim", what exactly does "Muslim" mean?

However, according to the common sense of modern society, a normal country should take "separation of politics and religion" and "separation of race and religion" as the basic institutional principles, and endow everyone with the right to choose and have their own religious beliefs as the free and independent individuals. In that case, according to this principle, the name "Muslim" can only refer to Islamists. Different from the country and race, the name "Muslim" should be specifically distinguished from the country and race.

However, nowadays, there are indeed a lot of conceptual confusions about the name of "Muslim", because in fact, the name seems to have become a feature of a conceptual ethnic group in the world today, which may be temporarily called a pan-national name. That is, there already exists the feature of using this pan-national name to bind religion to certain groups and even countries. This kind of pan-national name classifies the people who believe in their religion, which will bind the religious groups of the believers to a certain extent, and adversely affect the freedom of religious faith of individuals and related groups.

In addition, from the perspective of the world, the name "Muslim", which should be purely a religious concept name, has now become a pan-ethnic name, a name that is easy to be confused. If this confused concept causes people to regard it as a kind of national concept, it may have a negative impact on the integration of the relevant ethnic groups.

To sum up, we should unbind Islamists from the name "Muslim", that is, if a person or family believes in Islam, it should only be called an Islamist or Islamic family directly. It should not be called "Muslim", which is easy to cause conceptual confusion, so as to let religion return to religion and race to race. In other words, Islam is still Islam, all ethnic groups still have their own original national names, and everyone does not have pan-national names other than national names for religious reasons.

● One more thing to add:

Some people say that the word "Muslim" means a person who voluntarily obeys Allah, which means "Islamic". Thus, "Islamic" can be replaced by the name "Muslim". But in fact, the name "Muslim" now refers not only to Islamists, but also to Islamic countries and certain conceptual ethnic groups. Therefore, there has obviously been a lot of conceptual confusion, which has little to do with the meaning of Islam. As a result, Islam should return to Islam instead of deriving religious names involving countries and nationalities. Such the confusion is more obvious at present.

In other words, if the name "Muslim" can simply indicate that it is Islamic, and no longer involves the scope of countries and nationalities, then there is no problem with its use. But if it involves the scope of countries and nationalities, and is easy to cause conceptual confusion or even misleading, then I think it is better to call Islamists directly, instead of using "Muslim".

As for the name "Muslim", if some people are really keen on using it, it should only be used within the church rather than the external circle, just as Christian names such as "disciple" and "apostle" can only be used within the church. Otherwise, if another pan-national name is created in the world, it will only bring a negative impact on individual freedom of faith or national integration.

3. On The Status Quo of Islam From the Perspective of Freedom of Faith

In the past, people's understanding about freedom of faith was generally limited to the freedom of believing in and praising the religion, but they often lack a deep understanding about the freedom of not believing in and belittling the religion., thereby indicating their partial understanding about the freedom of faith. Thus, a more comprehensive understanding about the freedom of faith is missing.

That is to say, from the perspective of relatively complete freedom of faith, any normal religion itself must be able to allow everyone to freely choose to believe it or not, praise or belittle it, rather than just choose to believe in and praise it, but not freely choose to disbelieve and belittle it. Therefore, in this respect, if a religion allows only the freedom of one-way choice of believing in and praising the religion, but not the freedom of not believing in and belittling it, then there is no freedom of two-way choice. In other words, it is compulsive, and it is not a normal religious faith.

Moreover, what is the purpose of freedom of faith? It is to safeguard everyone's right to freedom of faith, that is, to endow everyone with the freedom to choose to believe in or not to believe in a religion, to praise or belittle a religion. The freedom of faith should never be just adopted to defend a religion.

Therefore, if we look at the status quo of Islam from the perspective of freedom of faith, we will find that the practices of the integration of politics and religion and ethnic and religious bundling in some Islamic countries fall into the practice of forced belief to a large extent. The integration of politics and religion requires the citizens to generally abide by the teachings according to the religious laws, and ethnic and religious bundling requires the ethnic groups to generally abide by the teachings in the name of the nation, which have in fact violated the relevant principles of freedom of faith.

In addition, as we know from some news and events, in these Islamic countries where politics and religion are integrated, their citizens generally lack the freedom of faith, and even some people have been required and punished by their religious laws because they have converted to other religions or fail to follow certain teachings, and some of them have even put their lives in danger. In fact, some of these phenomena have run counter to the individual principle of freedom of faith.

From the perspective of the world, Islamists should only be called Islamists, but the name "Muslim" used by them has now become a confused name between nationalities and religions, and has actually become a pan-national name. As a result, there has been a universal phenomenon of ethnic and religious binding with the pan-ethnic characteristics.

It can be seen from the above that there is only one-way free choice of faith in today's Islam in many places, but there is no normal two-way free choice of faith, which are some of the problems existing in Islam today.

Therefore, judging from these situations that exist in Islam today, when it comes to protecting the freedom of faith in Islam, what I want to say is that we should also pay attention to the need to urge the whole Islam to carry out relevant reforms. Because only after the universal separation of politics and religion, nationality and religion, Islam can become a normal religious faith that people can freely choose to believe in it or not, praise or belittle it. Then, ensuring their two-way freedom of faith can be called safeguarding their freedom of faith. Otherwise, the so-called protection of the relevant freedom of faith is only a kind of one-way freedom to safeguard some forced belief practices existing in the religion, but not to maintain the two-way freedom of religion for people to freely choose to believe in and praise it, and not freely choose to disbelieve and belittle it, then it is undoubtedly not worthwhile, and goes against the original intention of freedom of faith.

To sum up, under the environment of complete freedom of faith, any religion in a country does not have absolute freedom of faith, but only relative freedom of faith. In other words, any religion must be able to allow everyone to freely choose to believe it or not, praise or belittle it. If a religion becomes such a normal religion with free choice, and is thereby protected by national laws, then this is the real freedom of faith, making sense for all religions.

Chapter 4 On Details of The Rules on

Freedom of Faith

This chapter expounds the general rules on freedom of faith, clarifies and explains some controversial issues, and illustrates the relevant boundaries of the freedom of faith and the correct rules on the freedom of faith.

1. Is This the Forced Religion if Children Are Instructed to Believe in the Religion?

Nowadays, there are some people on the Internet who hold the idea that if children are instructed by their parents to believe in the religion, then it is the forced religion, because children do not have the ability to believe in the religion. Thus, is it a forced religion if children are instructed to believe in the religion? If so, then in fact, almost all religions today involve forced faith. Thus, if this problem is not clarified, it will bring a lot of unnecessary confusion to the essential difference between normal religion and forced religion.

1.   Parents' custody includes the right of religious guidance

We are aware that a child does not have the ability to choose to believe in the religion or not independently, but his or her parents have the right of custody, and this right of custody already includes the right to education. In addition, the right to education includes the right to guide the children regarding all cultures, such as national culture and religious culture. In other words, parents have priority in treating children's religious and cultural guidance, and parents have absolute right to guide their children to learn and accept their religious faith. In fact, this is the same as parents who do not have the religious faith but have the right to guide their children to learn and accept various cultures such as atheistic culture.

Some people have questioned that if parents have the right to guide their children's religion and culture, what should we do if some parents forced their children to believe in the religion? In fact, the answer to this question is very simple, because the family originally belongs to the private domain, and it is difficult for others to interfere with what is right and wrong within the family, unless it is really related to the specific illegal issue of domestic violence. This means, on the one hand, parents have the right of normal religious guidance, but such the right belongs to the private domain, and on the other hand, if parents violently force their children to believe in the religion for any reason (including possible religious faiths), then the country already has relevant anti-domestic violence laws or juvenile protection laws in place to protect them, and under such relevant legal protection, the country can punish the parents or even deprive them of their custody rights.

Thus, it can be seen that parents' religious guidance rights and forced faith practices are completely different in nature. Even if parents involve some violent coercion on their children during their lives (for possible religious reasons), such practice should only fall into the scope of domestic violence, but not fall into the scope of forced faith practice. Therefore, only the relevant anti-domestic violence laws or juvenile protection laws are needed to protect children. It can also be seen that the argument that parents force their under-age children to believe in the religion is actually a pseudo-proposition.

2.   Children themselves have the right to believe in the religion

Moreover, although children are under-age and do not have the ability to choose to believe in the religion independently, they still have the right to learn a religious culture or not. This right includes the right to believe in the religion or not under the guidance of their parents, as well as the right to choose to believe in the religion or not from a variety of circumstances. It can also be seen here that those who argue that children believing in the religion means the forced faith, which is also an opposition to the right of children to learn a certain religious culture or to profess a certain religion.

3.   Children's participation in religious rituals is no forced faith

With regard to children's religious faith, someone once asked me a question that, in the West, there are four-year-old children who receive religious baptism, while four-year-old children do not have any ability to discriminate between anything. Thus, such practice should fall into the scope of forced faith. My answer to this question is that, although the child is baptized at the age of four (including water baptism and possible immersion), the child can still choose to withdraw from the religion as he or she grows up. Because for those who do not believe in the religion, the superficial religious ritual is actually just a bath at most, and there is no harm at all. Therefore, the key is whether the child has the freedom to quit and change at any time is an important topic, and it is this key factor that defines whether it is forced faith or not.

4.   What is the force faith?

Then, what is forced faith? The true forced faith deprives the right of the freedom of withdraw from and convert the religion, and the freedom of criticizing and belittling the religion. In addition, the religious laws are implemented instead of national laws.

5.   Instructing the children to believe in the religion falls into the scope of freedom of faith

For instructing children to believe in the religion, children first believe in the religion under the religious guidance of their parents, falling into the private domain of the family. That is, it belongs to the scope of free and voluntary freedom of faith, and others have no right to interfere. Moreover, although children are under-age, they also have the right to learn religious culture and practice religion from their parents and surrounding people, and their rights to freedom of belief and learning cannot be deprived just because they are children.

In other words, for religious faith, parents have the right to guide, and children have the right to learn, thereby the two complementing each other to form a part of freedom of faith.

6.   Forced faith has nothing to do with the children

In addition, it should be noted that the above topic about children's freedom of faith naturally refers to all normal religions. However, for those religions that already have the practice of forced faith, the children have no freedom of withdrawing from and change the religion, and are deprived of the right of freedom of religious expression, after they believe in the religion. Then for such the religion, both children and adults are under the practice and scope of forced faith.

7.   Conclusion

To sum up, it can be seen that children's belief in religion does not fall into the category of forced faith. Only in the absence of freedom of withdrawing from and changing the religion, and the freedom of religious speech, then it is the true forced faith. Therefore, determining whether there is the forced faith practice cannot be judged by one's own personal likes and dislikes, but should be judged by rules. Only with rules, can we correctly distinguish the difference between normal religion and forced belief religion in terms of practice.

2. You Can Belittle the Religion, But Cannot Oppose the Religious Rights

Nowadays, it is often seen that many people are unable to distinguish between belittling religion and opposing religion rights, and mistakenly think that belittling the religion is tantamount to opposing the religion. Therefore, some practices against religion will also be mistakenly regarded as just a kind of belittling the religion, resulting in confusion and tolerance. However, if we look at this issue according to the relevant principles of freedom of faith, we will know that belittling the religion and opposing the religion are completely different in nature. Therefore, it is very important to clarify the difference between the two, so as to put an end to conceptual confusion, and therefore treat them differently.

1. Can the religion be belittled?

First of all, we have to ask: can the religion be belittled? The answer is of course yes. As we emphasized in the previous section of "freedom of religious expression", it is everyone's right to believe in and belittle a religion. Thus, it is acceptable for a person to criticize or even belittle a religion in speech, all of which fall within the scope of freedom of religious expression.

2. Can the religion be opposed?

Moreover, can we object to other people's right to profess a certain religion? The answer is of course no. Because as long as there is no forced faith in a religion, then such a religion is a normal religion. As we emphasized in the previous section of "freedom of religious expression", it's everyone's right to believe in and praise the normal religion, while others should only support and respect their rights.

In addition, in order to avoid some conceptual confusion among some people, there is a problem which needs to be specifically clarified here. Because someone asked, "is it okay if you personally reject and oppose a religion, but do not interfere with the rights of others to believe in the religion?" The answer to this question is that the so-called individual rejecting and opposing a religion actually means that one does not believe in and belittles a religion. However, this is different from publicly opposing a religion, because what we generally call anti-religion (rights) refers to the public nature of making demands on others (that is, involving the second person), which should be clearly distinguished.

3. Both the rights of believing in the religion or not should be supported

Thus, it is very important here that you have the right not to believe in and belittle a religion, but at the same time others also have the right to believe in and praise a religion. This is not to say that you have the right to disbelieve and belittle a religion, while others do not have the right to believe in and praise a religion. It can be seen that in the rules on freedom of faith, the right to believe in and the right not to believe in are equally important and should be supported and defended.

4. The religion with the practice of forced faith should be opposed

However, there is a religious practice that can be opposed. For example, if there are some forced belief practices in a religion, it itself violates the relevant principles of freedom of faith. Thus, it is no longer a normal religious belief practice. For such a religion which contains some forced faith practices, we should naturally urge it to reform, transforming it into a normal religious faith. Otherwise, if it is opposed by others because of some forced belief practices, in my opinion, it will be difficult find an excuse.

5. Opposing the normal religious rights is actually violating the rules

Today, we often see some people who oppose the legitimate rights of all religions, reflected in not only their opposition of forced religious faith, but also their opposition of normal religion. On the surface, they are right about the opposition of forced religious faith, but wrong about the opposition of normal religion. However, what I want to say about this is that they oppose all religions only on the basis of their personal likes and dislikes, disrupting the rules. In fact, they do not have a positive significance.

Since opposing religion on the basis of personal likes and dislikes without any rules already features autocratic thinking, relying on autocratic thinking rather than rules will only bring about a kind of confusion and destruction in rules, which actually binds all religions together and mixes them together. On the contrary, it will make it impossible for the people affected by it to distinguish the nature of religion.

Therefore, to a certain extent, when you violate the relevant principles of freedom of faith and oppose the legitimate rights of some normal religions, you are actually biased and indirectly supporting those abnormal religions.

6.   Opposing the force faith should be done by relying on the rules of freedom of faith

In the past, some people thought that opposing forced faith should rely on despotism, because from some practical phenomena, forced faith seems to be the natural enemy of democracy, and balancing it with despotism seems to be more direct and powerful than democracy. However, I don't think so now.

Since the autocratic thinking itself is arbitrary, it is easy to suppress normal religion according to personal likes and dislikes and interests, but it is also possible to tolerate forced faith in religion. As there is no institutional regularity, and its risk is huge, people cannot rely on the autocratic thinking.

As for the democratic system, although it is now easy to tolerate some practices of forced faith, it is only necessary to popularize the general knowledge about the relevant rules of freedom of faith to the public. After the public is generally aware of the fact that some religions in the world do have forced faith practices, then we can reach a consensus together and reasonably urge some of these religions to carry out reforms in accordance with the law, so as to remove the relevant forced belief practices.

It can be seen that opposing the practice of forced faith should still rely on the relevant rules on freedom of faith, not on the autocratic thinking of opposing the rules. Otherwise, it will be futile to disrupt the rules.

7. The relevant forced faith practices can be resolved with the rules

To sum up, the religion can be belittled, but at the same time it must support everyone's normal religious rights. As Voltaire once said: "disapprove of what you say, but I will defend to the death your right to say it." In other words, I do not believe in or belittle this normal religion, but I will defend to the death your right to practice this normal religion. In this way, the rules in some religions related to forced faith practices can be resolved naturally.

3. Religions That Cannot Be Criticized Have Certain Characteristics of Forced Faith

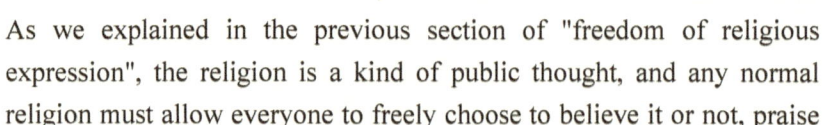

As we explained in the previous section of "freedom of religious expression", the religion is a kind of public thought, and any normal religion must allow everyone to freely choose to believe it or not, praise or belittle it (including criticism).

1. Religions that cannot be criticized have certain characteristics of forced faith

Therefore, if there is a religion that does not allow people to praise or criticize it freely (including belittling), it means that this religion has imposed certain restrictions on people's freedom of religious expression. In fact, it has violated the relevant principles of freedom of faith. More precisely speaking, it has a certain degree of compulsion to the people, and has certain characteristics of forced faith.

2. The reason why the freedom of belittling religion has not been recognized by the world yet

In fact, there are still many people who mistakenly believe that religion needs to be respected and cannot be criticized or belittled. The reason why they have such misunderstandings is mainly due to the lack of a correct understanding about the freedom of religious expression, and they do not know that respecting religion and respecting individual religious rights are two different things. Since they do not know that respect for people and respect for religion are completely different in nature, it results in some conceptual confusion.

In addition to the reasons for the above misunderstandings, there are other reasons why freedom of speech criticizing religion has not been widely recognized by the people of different religions in the past. It has influenced people's correct understanding of freedom of religious expression, which shows the relevant attitudes of the following three groups towards freedom of religious expression:

(1) Today's common Islamists oppose the criticism of Islam by others, and often threaten and interfere with those who criticize Islam.

(2) Some believers of Christianity, Buddhism and other religions do not like others to criticize their own religions. Thus, under the influence of personal religious sentiments, they tolerate and acquiesce to the freedom of speech of criticizing the religions to a certain extent. But this is certainly wrong.

(3) As for atheists, it is easier for them to accept and understand.

3. Islam involves the practice of anti-freedom of religious expression, which should be reformed

From the point of view of the above two groups of people, Islamists are generally opposed to criticizing Islam, and in fact, it is common to see Islamists threaten or even interfere with others, which is essentially the disallowance to be criticized. Thus, there is a certain degree of compulsion in these practices. In view of this, I think its opposition to freedom of religious expression should be reformed so that it can support the public right to freedom of religious expression.

4. Other religions do not involve the practice of anti- freedom of religious expression

As for Christianity, Buddhism and other religious believers, they just don't like others to criticize their own religions. Although recently, for example, people of a certain religion have made verbal protests against others' belittling their own religion, at present, it seems that it is only a verbal protest, and it is more like a kind of criticism, and it has not actually posed a real threat to others. Therefore, although it is a small mistake, there is no actual compulsion existing in such religions.

5. How should normal religions treat the criticism and belittling by others?

In addition, I would like to explain once again what kind of attitude normal religions should take towards the belittling by others. As I said in my previous discussion on "the difference between criticism and protest", in the face of other people's belittling, you can criticize and correct the others' erroneous remarks about belittling, which is your right to correct, but you do not have the right to protest. Instead, you should defend the other party's right to criticize and belittle the religion.

6.   The world should defend the freedom of religious expression

It can be said that freedom of religious expression forms the basis for the existence of all normal religions. The belief and praise of a religion is part of freedom of faith and freedom of religious expression, while the acceptance of disbelief and disparagement (including criticism) of a religion is also part of freedom of faith and freedom of religious expression.

Therefore, those who praise religions do not have the right of opposing others' speech of criticizing the religions, and those who criticize religions also do not have the right of opposing others' speech of praising the religions. To deny any of these rights here is to either produce either some kind of autocratic thinking or produce some kind of religious compulsion.

Therefore, the world should re-recognize the importance of freedom of religious expression, and national laws should also give strong protection to the people's right to the freedom of religious expression.

4. Can A Country Judge the Cult?

For this question, people usually hold two views. Some believes that there are indeed cults in the world, and it is appropriate for the government to take measures against it. Others believe that the country shall not become a religious tribunal. According to the principle of separation of politics and religion, whether a religion is pure or evil, it should fall within the scope of citizens' free choice. The country does not have the right to limit or judge citizens in the field of thought and religion. That is to say, the country does not have the power to judge cults.

On the surface, the above two views seem to be opposed to each other. But in fact, we only need to clarify their relevant views and clarify the rules of freedom of faith, then we can understand that the two views are not opposed to each other. Instead, the two views only talk about different aspects of the issue.

First of all, the government indeed has no right to arbitrarily judge whether a religion is a cult or not. In other words, the government does not have the right to judge a religious group as a cult on the basis of some people's subjective likes and dislikes. Otherwise, judging a thought or religion as a cult on the basis of subjective likes and dislikes will in fact violate the practice of freedom of faith and will give rise to practical restrictions on citizens' faith. Moreover, judging a thought or religion as a cult on the basis of subjective likes and dislikes has also violated the principle of separation of politics and religion, and it is obviously wrong to violate the principle of separation of politics and religion.

Then, does the government essentially have the right to judge a religion as an abnormal religion or a cult? Of course. It can be said that

43

when the doctrine of a religion has been advocated and has been involved in violating national laws, such as injuring people and killing lives, there will be a certain degree of harm to society. At this time, the government has the right to judge it as a cult to distinguish it from other normal religions. In other words, when the dogmatic propositions of a religion and the related acts arising from the implementation of its teachings have already violated the law, the country can regard it as a cult according to the relevant religion in which it violates the law. The relevant religious practices that violate the law are judged by law, which is also in line with the principle of separation of politics and religion.

Some people may worry that if the government can judge cults, it will have adverse consequences and may infringe upon citizens' freedom of faith. Of course, this worry is not unreasonable, and in fact, some autocratic countries are also adopting this approach. They suppressed many religious believers in the name of judging cults, causing many people to encounter difficulties. However, in the face of such a government's possible infringement of freedom of faith, we still have to say that we should not give up our guard against and understanding about real cults because of the erroneous practices by some governments. Instead, we should still recognize the need for the country to judge the true cults.

Here we must understand the possible harm by real cults to society. When the doctrine of a cult itself and related violence and other illegal issues are involved in its implementation, if the national law does not restrict it, then the cult will not perish of itself among religious competition, on the contrary, it will have a more competitive advantage against many normal religions, and will flourish. Because its relevant doctrinal propositions that violate national laws will make individual people feel helpless, the violent acts such as wounding and killing involved in the implementation of its teachings will have a certain psychological deterrent to the public. Eventually the society will gradually give in to them. If the cult is allowed to develop, people will actually be helpless.

This reason is actually very simple. For example, in a country, if a social organization's relevant claim involves the breach of law, then its claim will not dare to be publicized at all. Otherwise, the national law will restrict it. If some violent violations are actually involved, the national law will punish them and characterize them accordingly. By the same principle, such a social group should not be entitled to the privilege of immunity outside the law just because it is given extra protection in the name of religion. Thus, what it means here is that both general social groups and religious groups are equal in front of the national law. Since the law can characterize general social groups, religious groups can also be characterized.

Therefore, it can be seen that the statement that the country cannot judge a cult is not entirely correct. Because although the country cannot judge whether a religion is an evil cult according to the subjective likes and dislikes of some people, it can still be judged on the basis of some religious propositions and violations of national laws.

Here we also need to add a very important point. That is, when a country judges a religion to be a cult for violating the law, can individual believers be punished for this? The answer is No. Because the treatment of individuals here should still be in accordance with the principle of law. That is, the mind is innocent. Of course, a member of a cult who has not violated the law should not be punished by the law, and only when he violates the law can the country have the right to impose sanctions in response to his violation of the law. In other words, although the country can define a religion as a cult according to some religious practices that violate the law, individual believers must still be treated as normal citizens and can only be punished according to whether their external behavior violates the law or not. Their treatment should not be directly related to whether they believe in cults or not. Otherwise, the country is tantamount to infringing upon their personal freedom of faith.

To sum up, it can be seen that a country does not have the right to judge whether a religion is a cult on the basis of subjective likes and dislikes, but when the relevant religious practices of a religion have obviously violated national laws and caused obvious harm to society, the country has the right to judge it as a cult and exercise certain control over it. However, for specific individual believers, the government does not have the right to impose legal sanctions, and for individual believers, only when they have directly violated the law, the country has the right to impose corresponding sanctions on their violations of the law.

Therefore, it can be seen that even if the country can judge a religion as a cult on the basis of violation of the law, it has no right to impose sanctions on individual believers when their behavior does not violate the law.

Chapter 5 Illustration of Market Rules of

Religious Products

Although the relevant religious products market rules mentioned in this chapter are illustrated by Islamic halal food as an example, the relevant religious products of other religions are the same and apply the same principles.

1. About the Positioning of Halal Food

We all know that the so-called halal food is out of the teachings of Islam, based on which many Islamists often demand and interfere with halal food products on the market, believing that halal food should be supervised and licensed. But, on the other hand, many people think that it is an illegal act to interfere with secular society in the name of religion. Therefore, how to position halal food has become a highly controversial issue which may easily cause social contradictions.

As the controversy about halal food has touched all levels of society, this article also discusses the relevant aspects, in order to explain what kind of relevant principles halal food should follow in the secular society, and to define the correct position of halal food.

1.   The government has no right to characterize the halal food

Halal food is derived from the doctrine of Islam, and religion belongs to the category of public thought. Thus, the so-called "halal food" belongs to the category of public thought and belongs to the scope of the public's free understanding and acceptance of the teachings of Islam. Then, according to the principle of separation of politics and religion, the government does not have the right to use laws and regulations to define the relevant interpretation and authority of halal doctrine. This is just like the government does not have the right to define the Christian Christmas goods, and only the principles of market economy like Christmas goods should apply.

2.   Halal food does not have the right to register as the exclusive right to use a trademark

Since halal food belongs to the scope of religious teachings and has spread widely, it is neither registered as a trademark, nor is owned by certain people or some religious groups. Such religious words, like the general words in the trademark, are not allowed to be registered. This is just like the Christian principle that "Christmas" cannot be registered. Otherwise, if it is registered, it may be controlled by some people, which is tantamount to monopolizing a certain aspect of the doctrine. In other words, according to legal principles, any individual or group does not have private ownership of the word "halal". Instead, it belongs to the general scope of society.

3. Halal food is not privately owned by any individual or religious group

It can be seen from the above that halal food belongs to the category of religious doctrine, and religion belongs to the scope of public thought. Thus, the word "halal" as a religious doctrine should belong to everyone (including non- Islamists), and everyone has the right of free interpretation and free use of it. It does not belong to any individual or religious group, and any individual or religious group does not have the right to monopolize the power of interpretation to interfere in how others use it.

4. For halal diet, only individuals can make demands on themselves

Therefore, there is a very important principle of religious belief here. That is, all normal religious beliefs are individual religious beliefs, and their compliance with the teachings should only be the demands of believers on themselves rather than on others. Then the halal diet belongs to the religious category, which means that each believer is free to choose whether he or she is willing to abide by it or not, and he or she has no right to demand and interfere with each other. This should be especially true in dealing with the outside secular society. Therefore, if we put too much emphasis on halal in the secular society, it is a violation of the freedom of others and of the secular world.

5. Whether a kind of halal food is authentic should be determined by the market principle of selecting the superior and eliminating the inferior

Then some people may ask, if everyone in the world is free to understand and use the name of halal food, will Islamists then be unable to eat authentic halal food?

To solve this problem, it is actually very simple. The answer is to let the market return to the market. Whether a kind of halal food is authentic or not, there will be Islamists who freely choose to buy halal food so that the market will select the superior and eliminate the inferior. However, if there are Islamists who claim to interfere with halal food that they consider to be unauthentic, their right to interference is limited to their own personal non-purchase of halal food, but they do not have the right to have opinions or complaints about such merchants, and merchants cannot force Islamists to purchase halal food in the name of halal food. Every Islamists should be given the right to choose and buy freely.

In other words, although every merchant has the right to sell what he thinks is halal food, Islamists also have the right to choose the authentic halal food in their opinion. In this way, the rights of both merchants and Islamists are guaranteed. By letting the market select the superior and eliminate the inferior, we just need to follow the principles of market economy.

6.   Religious organizations have no right to require Islamists to eat halal food

Some people asked me whether some religious organizations in Islam have the right to expel an Islamist if he or she does not eat halal food. In this regard, I think that religious organizations should only advocate the religious diet of believers and have no right to interfere. However, if an Islamic organization expels an Islamists just because of the doctrine of diet, then the Islamists also have the right to choose other Islamic organizations and have the right not to join any Islamic organization.

In other words, religious belief belongs to individual religious belief. Whether a believer is willing to eat halal food is a question about whether he or she is pious or how pious he or she is. A normal religious organization may thereby interfere with the rise and fall of his or her status within the organization, but it has no right to interfere with the freedom of choice of his or her personal belief.

7. Conclusion

To sum up, it can be seen that normal religious faiths are personal religious faiths, and whether an Islamist is willing to abide by the teachings of halal food should only be out of his or her own requirements. However, he or she has no right to make demands on others and the outside world. And even if Islamists are required to abide by the doctrine of halal food in a religious organization, individuals have the right to choose whether they want to do so or not. In other words, according to the rules on freedom of faith, all people (including Islamists and non- Islamists) have their own personal freedom to understand and choose halal food, and no individual or organization has the right to interfere with it.

Postscript:

Do public places need to take care of the halal needs of Islamists?

1. Is it necessary to set up halal places for the religion in public places?

Nowadays, some Islamists require schools, airports and other public places to set up halal restaurants in the name of their own religious beliefs, but this is of course an unreasonable requirement. Because all normal religions belong to the scope of individual religious faith, a person who believes in a religion should demand himself rather than others by doctrine, and should bear the burden of abiding by the doctrine rather than asking others to bear it. Otherwise, it will bring about a dogmatic demand on society. Because the religion belongs to the scope of public thought, the believers have chosen to abide by the ideological requirements of a certain doctrine, which is their own choice of religious will, and they should naturally bear the requirements of their own teachings. If others may also choose to help them, they should also be grateful for this, but understand that public society is not responsible for the demands arising from their belief in and observance of a religious doctrine.

2.   Halal food belongs to the scope of religion, not folk-custom

For the above, it has been argued that halal food has become a folk custom in some areas. Thus, public places should have the duty to take care of it. My answer is that religion belongs to religion and folk-custom belongs to folk-custom, both of which are two categories. If halal food has become the category of folk-custom, then religion can no longer have any doctrinal interference with folk food. If it is in the category of religion, it can only be the Islamist individuals who ask themselves to do it, not ask others to do it. If the two are bound to each other, that is, it is both a religious category and a folk-custom category, then there is a requirement of secularity with religious teachings. That is, there is a certain compulsion to the secular society. However, according to today's facts, halal food is actually out of the teachings of Islam and is widely used among Islamists. Thus, there is no doubt that it belongs to the category of religion.

3.   There is no obligation in public places to abide by a religious doctrine

Thus, it can be seen that public places are not responsible for the obligations of a certain religious doctrine. Otherwise, if public places need to bear the requirements of the halal doctrine of Islam, then Buddhists can also ask for vegetarian canteens in public places, and Christianity also requires prayer rooms set up in public places, which will be absurd. Therefore, it can be seen that religion belongs to personal religious beliefs, and the observance of a religious doctrine should be based on the principle of personal burden, rather than requiring others or public places to bear their obligations to abide by religious teachings.

2. The Religious Doctrine Interpretation of Religious Products Falls Into the Category of Public Thought

We know that the so-called religious products generally refer to the products made by an interpretation of the corresponding religious teachings. Then, when we understand the relevant rules of freedom of belief, and understand some correct definitions of religion and its related religious names in the public society, we will naturally be able to understand what the market rules of religious products should be like in the public society.

1. The religion belongs to the scope of public thought

As I have stated earlier, religion is a kind of public thought, and anyone has the right to praise or belittle any religion freely, as well as has the right to freely choose to believe it or not, and is free to choose to change these relevant perceptions and understandings at any time, regardless of whether they are religious believers or not.

2. The religion cannot be privately owned

Therefore, since religion belongs to a kind of public thought, it is different from specific people and things, and cannot become personal private property. Believers have no right to possess a certain religious thought, and those who do not believe also have no right to possess a certain religious thought, which means that no one has the right to monopolize and possess a religion, and has no right to require others to understand and comply with a religious doctrine in the same way as they do, regardless of whether they are religious believers or not.

3. The definition of religious believers

The so-called religious followers refer to the recipients of certain religious ideas. In other words, if a person believes and praises a religious thought, he can be said to be the recipient of that religious thought. However, praising and accepting a religious thought does not mean that it is a private property.

Therefore, for each religious believer, religion can only be his or her personal belief, and he or she can only choose to praise and believe a certain religion, but cannot ask others to praise and believe it. You can only understand a religious doctrine and ask yourself to do so, but not to understand a religious doctrine and ask others to follow it.

4.   The definition of a religious community (or organization, the same below)

The so-called religious community is composed of a certain number of religious believers. In other words, some people who have the same understanding and acceptance of a certain religious idea. To put it more simply, the religious community is made up of some people with the same values, which is the same as the general community in society, and there is no fundamental difference.

Then it can be seen that the religious community, like the general community, is a kind of community organization established under the national law, and its management authority is limited to its internal management affairs such as the rise and fall of the status of believers. As for the understanding and acceptance of a religious idea by its community, it can be regarded as its community values, which can manage the rise and fall of the status of its followers according to its values. However, it is limited to this, and does not have the right to impose some punishment on its religious members that go beyond the national laws.

Similarly, every religious believer can choose to join his or her favorite religious community in accordance with his own understanding of a certain religious idea and personal values, and has the right to change at any time in accordance with his or her own values, as well as has the right to choose to withdraw from a religious community and join other societies at any time.

To sum up, it can be seen that the religious community only has the right to manage the internal affairs of the community under the national law, and does not have the right to claim a certain religion as private property on the basis of its understanding of a certain religious thought, and to make doctrinal demands on a certain religious believer. What's more, the religious community has no right to put forward doctrinal requirements to people outside the community and society on the basis of its understanding of a certain religious thought.

5.　Associated legal rights of religious community

Religious communities, like ordinary societies in society, may register their own independent relevant trademarks according to the values of their own societies, carry out some commercial operations, and authorize the doctrinal products and merchants that conform to the values of their own communities, namely, the possible authoritative certification of a product, so that relevant believers and the public can choose and buy authentic products that conform to the values of their own communities.

6.　Can religious products violate religious teachings?

Here we would like to talk about the question of whether religious products can violate religious teachings. But in fact, this is actually a pseudo-proposition.

Because anyone can freely understand a religious doctrine and have freedom of speech to praise or belittle it. Then anyone has the right to understand a religious product freely, even at will, and there is no question of whether a religious product violates the religious doctrine.

To be more specific, anyone's understanding of a religious doctrine is free and flexible. Then, to what extent a religious product should be strictly observed can be regarded as the conformance of doctrine? There are various opinions among various people. Some people may be more strict, some people may be more casual, and everyone's understanding is different. Thus, who has the right to define a certain religious doctrine and even a religious product? In my opinion, only the gods of religion have the right to define it, thereby it is not operable.

Therefore, according to the relevant principle of separation of politics and religion, the national law cannot interfere in the affairs of the relevant religious products, but only need to allow the trademark authorization and certification management of the relevant religious organizations, and let the relevant religious products follow the principle of market economy. Whether the religious products are authentic or not can be determined by the free choice of purchase by the relevant believers and the public.

For those merchants who do not allow a religious community to license the trademark, can they also freely sell religious products? Yes, of course. Because, as mentioned earlier, religious teachings are not private property, and no one has the right to interfere with the manufacturing of products by others with a certain religious doctrine that they understand. The right to object is only limited to their decision of buying such products. Thus, whether such products are authentic or whether people are willing to buy such religious products is based on the principle of market economy.

7.   The composition of food is different from that of religious products

Someone once asked me about the question of "meat and vegetables", saying that if some products were marked with vegetables but the meat was sold, wouldn't this be a kind of advertising fraud involving religious products? My answer to this is: "meat and vegetable" is actually an adjective for food ingredients, not a freely understandable definition of religious products. That is to say, mislabeling of food ingredients can involve advertising fraud. However, national laws should not interfere with the religious products that are in line with religious teachings, but should follow the principle of separation of politics and religion, which is a boundary that must be strictly distinguished.

8.   The integration of normal religion and secularity

Therefore, if we can follow the principle that religion belongs to public thought rather than private property, then a normal religion will naturally integrate into the secular society: its relevant religious name may become a secular name, religious festivals may become secular festivals, religious products may become secular products, and their related religious names will only become a cultural symbol and related secular festivals and products.

What is different from the above normal religious practice is that the religion with the practice of forced belief treats religion as private property and puts forward requirements to the secular society with religious teachings. As a result, it is difficult for the relevant religious names to integrate into the secular society, and the relevant religious products are difficult to become secular products and become exclusive to religious believers. If they make such religious dogma requirements on the secular society, it may bring a lot of social contradictions.

9.   Conclusion

To sum up, religion belongs to a kind of public thought, everyone has the right to understand any religion freely, and the dogmatic interpretation of religious products belongs to the scope of everyone's free understanding. Therefore, for the market operation of religious products, the country should follow the principle of separation of politics and religion, and protect the principle of market freedom of relevant religious products by law. We should not interfere with the principle of market freedom of relevant religious products on the basis of some people's understanding of a religious doctrine.

3. Religious Products Cannot Become A Requirement of Religious Law

Nowadays, some Islamists think that some merchants' products do not meet the requirements of halal teachings on the grounds that halal food must be authentic, and put pressure on and interfere with some merchants. Some related stores were even smashed. Such a practice of making demands on society with religious teachings is in fact a manifestation of making demands to society with religious laws, which actually violates the relevant principles of freedom of belief.

However, some people think that merchant products that do not meet the requirements of halal doctrine are at fault and should be interfered with. In fact, the reason why some people have such a misunderstanding is that they do not have a clear understanding of the separation of religions and customs, they do not understand religious teachings cannot replace national laws, and there are still a large number of people who hold such misunderstandings and thereby tolerate the existence of such implemented religious laws to a certain extent. Therefore, I think it is necessary to clarify the nature and existence of such relevant religious laws in order to make the public aware of and alert to this.

1. What is the religious law?

In short, the religious law is to make demands to society on the basis of religious teachings rather than national laws. In other words, any request to the society based on religious doctrine is essentially the implementation of religious law, which is a law other than the national law. I think the country should be vigilant about this.

2. What is the normal practice of religious faith:

The normal practice of religious belief is different. According to the principle of freedom of belief, no matter what religion he believes in, anyone can only demand himself according to the religious doctrine he believes in, but not others with the religious doctrine. This right to ask others includes no right to make demands on fellow believers, and no right to make demands on non-believers, let alone to make demands on society, but only on their own individuals in terms of religious teachings.

3.   Anyone who understands any religious doctrine has the same right to freedom:

As we emphasized earlier, the religion is a kind of public thought, while its public nature will not change because of anyone's belief. In addition, the religion belongs to the scope of the right that everyone in the world can freely understand and accept it. Therefore, for any religious doctrine, any believer and non-believer have the same right of freedom to understand, and even to praise or belittle it. With regard to this right to freedom of belief, I think any country should provide legal protection to every citizen.

4.   The religious products should follow the principle of market economy:

Therefore, for the religious teaching products of a certain religion, every merchant is free to produce the product according to the teachings he or she understands, or even to produce the products without the doctrine itself. No one has the right to interfere with the production right of this free understanding. As for whether the products are in line with religious teachings, or whether they are authentic religious products, we can just let the market select the superior and eliminate the inferior.

For example, for Christian Christmas, Christians do not have the right to interfere with a merchant's Christmas tree on the grounds that it does not meet the requirements of the Bible. If an individual wants to buy a Christmas tree, he or she can choose a merchant that meets the requirements of the Bible in his or her opinion. That is, he or she only needs to buy it according to his or her own preferences and follow the principle of market economy.

Buddhist statues and items are another example. Buddhists do not have the right to interfere on the grounds that the statues and items of a certain merchant are not in line with Buddhist teachings. If individuals want to buy Buddha statues and items, they only need to choose the merchants that they think are in line with the teachings of Buddhism. That is, they only need to buy the products according to their own personal preferences and follow the principles of market economy.

By the same token, when it comes to Islamic halal food, Islamists do not have the right to interfere with a merchant's products that do not conform to the teachings of Islam. If individuals want to buy halal products, they can choose the merchants that they think are in line with the teachings of Islam. That is, they only need to buy the products according to their own personal preferences and follow the principles of market economy.

5.   Religious believers only have the right to demand merchants on the basis of whether the ingredients of the products are fake or not:

Therefore, according to the principle of market economy, no religious believers have the right to make demands on merchants' products with religious teachings, but they can demand merchants with relevant laws on whether the ingredients of the products are fake or not.

For example, if a product marked halal, even if it contains pork ingredients, then it does not involve the scope of falsification, because its ingredients have been marked. This falls within the scope of merchants' free understanding of halal and free production, and no one has the right to interfere with it.

However, if there is a product (whether it is marked halal or not), if the pork ingredient or a certain ingredient is deliberately hidden, then it falls into the scope of ingredient falsification, and the buyer can claim from the merchant in accordance with the relevant consumer protection law, but his or her claim is limited to this.

In this regard, if some Islamists think that merchants' product components are fraud, it is difficult to compensate for their personal mental loss only in accordance with the relevant consumer protection law. But the problem here is that as a normal consumer, you can only make a claim in accordance with the relevant legal principles of the country. The basis of the claim is the same as that of other citizens, and religious faith do not give believers additional special rights.

6. Religious law is mainly manifested in two forms:

At present, religious law is generally manifested in two forms: the first is that some religious groups or societies put forward doctrinal requirements to the society, such as the aforementioned religious teaching requirements of religious products on the market. The second is the relevant regulations on the management of religious commodities formulated by the country, such as some halal food regulations, which can also be regarded as a practice of putting forward doctrinal requirements to the society.

In fact, these two forms can be regarded as the performance of the requirements of the people on the basis of religious teachings, which is naturally wrong according to the relevant principles of freedom of belief and should be opposed. All religious products should follow the principle of market economy.

Chapter 6 Some Problems of Forced Faith

Existing in Islam

By comparing Islam with some religions, this chapter points out that there are some problems of forced faith existing in Islam in many aspects, and also explains what the relevant rules of freedom of belief should be, and how to deal with such problems correctly.

1. Some Forced Faith Practices Existing in Islam Are Different From Other Religions

In the above chapters, I have clearly pointed out the problems of the integration of politics and religion and ethnic and religious bundling that do exist in Islam in some places, thereby illustrating some forced belief practices that do exist today. In fact, such practices have violated the relevant principles of freedom of faith, which are essentially different from those of other religious faiths.

1. It is necessary to clarify the normal religious nature of Catholicism and Judaism

There are still many people who think that there seem to be other religions in the world that implement the integration of politics and religion, ethnic and religious bundling, and it is not just Islam that has this problem. As a result, it seems that they have chosen to ignore or tolerate these forced faith practices that exist in Islam today.

Therefore, I think it is necessary to mention the two religions which are easy to be misunderstood in the past, in order to explain their religious nature and characteristics, and to make a relevant comparison and explanation.

For these two religions, one is Catholicism, which has been easily mistaken by the world for the existence of the integration of politics and religion, and the other is Judaism, which has been easily mistaken for the existence of ethnic bundling in the past. However, according to the facts today, there is actually no practice of forced belief in these two religions, which is different from some practices of the integration of politics and religion and ethnic and religious bundling that exist in Islam today, which will be explained as follows.

2.   Catholicism does not involve the integration of politics and religion

Nowadays, many people think that Catholicism involves the integration of politics and religion. On the surface, this seems to be the case, but in fact it is not.

First of all, from the influence of its religion on individuals, today's Catholicism does not actually impose forced belief on individuals, and if its followers convert or violate their teachings or even put forward different doctrinal understandings, Catholicism will not and does not have the right to punish them politically and legally for this.

Moreover, judging from the influence of its religion on its relevant groups, if there is a Catholic group in a certain country in the world that does not recognize the authority of the Vatican pope, this group still has its freedom. The utmost the Vatican can do is not to recognize the authenticity of this group, but does not have the right to impose political and legal penalties on it.

Thus, it can be seen that on the surface, the Vatican is a country in the world, but in fact it can still be regarded as a cathedral and the exclusive right to use the Vatican trademark. All it can do are limited to its own religious affairs, and does not involve the political and legal personal punishment. Therefore, although many people may mistakenly think that it involves the integration of politics and religion, in fact, Catholicism today does not involve any practice of forced belief and does not have the essential characteristics of the integration of politics and religion, indicating that it is a normal practice of religious belief.

3.   Judaism does not involve the ethnic and religious bundling

Nowadays, many people think Judaism belongs to the Jewish people, and believe the Jewish nation and Judaism are tied together because both names are the same word "Jewish". But in fact, the two belong to two categories, that is, nationality belongs to nationality, religion belongs to religion, and the two are separated.

First of all, in today's Israel, the Jewish nation is mainly divided by descent, but Judaism is divided voluntarily. Within Israel, Jews have their own personal freedom even if they do not believe in Judaism, and others have no right to force them. Thus, in Israel, Judaism is not compulsive, and its separation of nationality from religion is obvious.

Moreover, there are people who believe in Judaism in other parts of the world, but they will only be called Jews, instead of being called Jews just because they believe in Judaism. In addition, individuals can even have the right to voluntarily withdraw from Judaism at any time without compulsion. It can also be seen that Judaism is a purely personal religious belief, and its separation of nationality from religion is also obvious.

In response to this, some people may say that the proportion of Jewish people who practice Judaism is higher than that of other ethnic groups, which should be regarded as ethnic and religious bundling. But this view is of course wrong, because every country or nation in the world has its own national culture and the right to advocate its own national culture. As long as there is no compulsion for a country to advocate its national culture, it all belongs to normal cultural advocacy. This is just like in my country, namely China, although there is a relatively concentrated Confucian cultural atmosphere, it cannot be said that there is Confucian cultural compulsion. Therefore, even if the proportion of Jewish people who believe in Judaism is relatively high, it still belongs to everyone's free will of religious belief. So long as there is no compulsion, it has nothing to do with ethnic and religious bundling.

4. The religious practices of Catholicism and Judaism are different from those of Islam

To sum up, it can be seen that today's Catholicism does not have the practice of forced belief, which means that there is no substantial nature of the integration of politics and religion, which should be a normal practice of religious belief. Similarly, there is no practice of forced belief in Judaism. Although the country can advocate Jewish (religious) culture, it is not forced. Thus, there is no ethnic and religious binding, which is also a normal practice of religious belief.

66

Compared with the two mentioned above, there is indeed a lot of confusion between Islamic rules and national laws in some Islamic countries. If someone violates the doctrine and converts in these countries, they may encounter the problem of legal punishment and even interference by others, and there is a considerable degree of political and religious integration. In addition, the "Muslim" name of its Islamic identity has actually become a kind of pan-national name, which has a certain degree of group binding. As a result, within the "Muslim" pan-national name group, there are religious teaching requirements for each other, and it can be seen that its ethnic and religious binding practice actually exists.

5.   Islam should be reformed to become a normal religious belief for everyone to choose freely

It can be seen, compared with Judaism, which used to be mistakenly believed that there is an integration of politics and religion, and Judaism, which used to be mistakenly believed that the ethnic and religious bundling exists, Islam does have a considerable degree of problems of the integration of politics and religion and ethnic and religious bundling. Therefore, it is different from other religions, including Catholicism and Judaism. As a result, I think Islam should reform such problems so as to become a religion with the separation of politics and religion, nationality and religion, that is, an individual religious belief that everyone can freely choose to believe it or not, praise or belittle it.

2. Some Views on Islamic Women Wearing Headscarves

In the impression of many people, Islamic women wearing headscarves seems to be a kind of national dress. But in fact, it is not, because wearing headscarves is not only the compliance with the provisions of Islamic teachings for female Islamists, but also widely used in many Islamic countries and Islamists, which shows that they belong to religious costumes, not national costumes.

Then, since wearing a headscarf is a religious dress, we can say that even according to the teachings of Islam, religious clothing should only be required for clergy and believers to wear in religious places, and ordinary women should not be forced to wear it in daily life. Even for national costumes, people have the right to freely choose whether to wear them in their daily life, let alone the religious clothing.

However, from some facts, it is a normal phenomenon that in some Muslim areas, especially in some Islamic countries, women will be discriminated against if they do not wear headscarves in their daily life, and may even be interfered by others. Thus, it can be seen that this religious dress now has certain characteristics of religious compulsion, and it is a fact that exists in some parts of the world.

In response to this, as some Islamists have retorted that some female Islamists wear headscarves voluntarily, it cannot be regarded as the forced characteristic clothing. But this argument is logically untenable, because according to normal logic, wearing headscarves is under the premise of a generally coercive environment that exists in quite a number of places, then it cannot be said that some women wear headscarves voluntarily. It can only be said that all women wear headscarves voluntarily only after many Islam countries and concentrated areas generally have the freedom for women not to wear headscarves.

In response to this, I would like to say to female Islamists who live in secular areas that when it is common in some parts of the world where women may be discriminated against and compelled to wear headscarves if they do not wear headscarves, then although it is a kind of personal freedom for you to wear headscarves in secular safe areas, it should not form a response to and support for those areas where wearing headscarves is mandatory. In other words, although wearing headscarves in secular areas is a kind of personal freedom, we must also criticize some practices in those areas where headscarves are generally enforced, in order to show that they wear headscarves out of their own personal freedom, and it has nothing to do with those places where wearing headscarves is mandatory.

In addition, I have seen some Islamists who praise the beauty of women wearing headscarves on the Internet. In my opinion, their praise is actually a paranoid guide, because according to the logic of normal people, praising the beauty of women should be to praise the beauty of people rather than to praise the beauty of headscarves, and whether a person is beautiful after wearing a headscarf varies from person to person. It can be seen that only praising the beauty of the headscarf is basically to support the religious compulsory characteristics of clothing. In fact, it is to put shackles on women's freedom of dress. Thus, I am critical of this kind of praise.

To sum up, we should all recognize that female Islamists wearing headscarves are not wearing national costumes but actually religious costumes, and we should criticize the compulsory characteristics of wearing headscarves in some Islamic countries, instead of choosing to ignore this phenomenon, in order to safeguard the basic right of all women (especially female Islamists) for the freedom of wearing.

3. The Definition of Moderate Muslims

(Islamists)

We know that all normal religions can only be individual religious beliefs, and it is important that Muslims can only refer to individual Islamists, not any nation or country.

Since there are some related religious conflicts in the world today, the world has a moderate view of individual Islamists. Then, what is a moderate Islamist, and how should the characteristics be defined? In my opinion, many people are superficial on this question, but if they really want to be serious about it, they cannot give the specific answer.

Therefore, this article will explain what moderate Islamists are according to the relevant principles of freedom of belief, and make a reasonable definition of the characteristics of moderate Islamists as far as possible.

1. Verbal anti-extremes does not mean moderate Islamists

Nowadays, many people have a misconception that an Islamist may be a moderate Islamist as long as he or she opposes the religious extremes verbally, but such an understanding is obviously too simple and superficial, because whether a person is a moderate Islamist or not, we should not simply look at whether he or she opposes religious extremes, but whether he or she supports the basic human rights of freedom of belief. This can be seen from whether he or she opposes the relevant forced belief practices and whether he or she holds the correct attitude towards freedom of religious belief.

2. The definition of moderate Islamists

Since moderate Islamists should have a correct attitude towards freedom of religious faith, they are bound to support the relevant principles of freedom of faith, such as: 1. identify with religious freedom of speech, agree that everyone has the right to freely choose to praise or belittle any religion; 2. recognize that everyone has the right to freely choose to believe in or not to believe in any religion (including withdrawal and conversion). 3. oppose the enforcement of religious laws instead of national laws.

Based on the above points, we recognize the dignity of national laws, and thereby oppose the implementation of religious laws that exist in some places of Islam, as well as the integration of politics and religion, ethnic and religious bundling and other related practices.

3.   Moderate Islamists should be distinguished not according to the appearance of kindness, but according to the practical attitude

Then, based on the above definition of moderate Islamists, whether an Islamist is moderate or not should not be distinguished by the superficial kindness, but by the practical attitude. For example, if an Islamist supports religious law, opposes freedom of withdrawal and conversion, and opposes freedom of religious speech, but appears to speak gently and kindly, then he is not a moderate Islamist. On the other hand, if an Islamist opposes religious law, supports freedom of withdrawal and conversion, and supports freedom of religious speech, but expresses his ideas in an irritated manner, then he can still be regarded as a moderate Islamist.

4.   Those who support democracy but do not oppose the practice of forced belief cannot be regarded as moderate Islamists

At present, many people tend to distinguish whether a person is a moderate Islamist out of the surface rather than the essence. For example, on the topic of democracy, I have seen some Islamists who do not object to the freedom of non-withdrawal and conversion and the widespread application of religious laws in some countries in the Middle East, but on the other hand, they call for local democracy and freedom, and some people are even called opinion leaders because of this.

However, according to the correct logic, since an Islamist is in Islam, he has no objection to the non-freedom of withdrawal and conversion from Islam in some countries, and has no objection to the implementation of Islam religious laws in these countries, then giving local democracy and freedom claimed by him is in fact tantamount to allowing the local religious law to take act freely, or to confuse local national laws and religious laws. Therefore, this voice does not certainly represent a moderate Islamist.

5.   The should-be attitude of moderate Islamists

On the other hand, the true moderate Islamists are bound to support the relevant principles of freedom of belief, that is, to support the basic human rights of every Islamists to have the freedom to withdraw and convert from Islam, to oppose religious laws, and to support the separation of politics and religion, separation of nation and religion, and to support every Islamists so that they can freely choose and have their own right to religious belief.

6.   The true moderate Islamists should be supported

Thus, I think for all people, we should re-recognize the relevant rules of freedom of belief, be vigilant to those who support the relevant forced belief practices, and give protection and support to those who are really moderate, in order to urge the relevant reform of Islam as a whole, and thereby remove some of the forced faith practices that exist in many parts of the world.

7.   The principles described in this article also apply to all religions

Although this article refers to the definition of moderate Islamists, the same principles can still be applied to all religions. That is, if there are forced belief practices in a religion, such as freedom of withdrawal and conversion, the enforcement of religious laws, then it is the responsibility of the religious followers to oppose some of these religious practices, rather than to become supporters of these religious practices.

4. What is the Society of the Integration of Politics and Religion

Nowadays, there are some Islamic groups (or organizations, the same below) in the world that make demands on the people of their countries with religious teachings, such as banning alcohol and pork in some places, censoring halal food, and others. With regard to these requirements, some people think that they should respect their religious beliefs and make concessions to them by constraining themselves. However, for such demands, some local people affected by these demands feel that the living space has been compressed, and the rights of individual freedom have been violated, thereby holding an attitude of opposition. Thus, how should we treat these groups that make demands to the public with religious teachings? This article will clarify this according to the relevant logic and facts.

1.   Normal religious associations should be part of civil societies

For a country, any religious community, like other societies, should only belong to a part of many civil societies, but can only claim the rights under the national law (such as the right to freedom of belief, etc.) as a civil society, which belongs to the nature of a normal religious community.

2.   A society with the integration of politics and religion is not part of a civil society

However, if a religious community make demands with religious teachings, rather than with the nature of a civil society, to obtain legitimate rights under national law (such as the right to freedom of belief, etc.), it is tantamount to breaking away from the nature of a civil association and has the characteristics of a community with the integration of politics and religion.

Thus, it can be seen that normal religious communities demand rights under national laws, while political and religious societies demand rights externally in terms of religious teachings, rather than as citizens' associations, making it a religious compulsion. I think the country should exercise some control on this issue.

3. The doctrinal requirements arising from the integration of politics and religion

(1) To make doctrinal demands on the people:

Since the society with the integration of politics and religion makes demands on the people with religious teachings, it will naturally feel the sense of compulsion brought about by certain doctrinal requirements for the non-religious groups where they are located. For example, in some Islamic countries and some secular countries, Islamists are prohibited from selling alcohol, pork and others. But with regard to such practices, we know that drinking and eating pork are the basic rights of every citizen. Thus, from these practices we can see the actual existence of the society with the integration of politics and religion, as well as some coercive practices on the people.

In addition, politico-religious societies also exert compulsion on some of the Islamists. For example, those who hold different understandings of the relevant teachings and those who are reluctant to worship the Islam will also feel a certain compulsion because of the actual existence and requirements of the society with the integration of politics and religion, thus depriving the individual's right to freely understand religious teachings and choices.

(2) To impose doctrinal requirements on the country:

Since the society with the integration of politics and religion requires the people with religious teachings. That is, for a group with the nature of the integration of politics and religion, when its group power becomes increasingly powerful, not only will the people feel compulsion, but also will the group inevitably begin to make doctrinal demands on the whole country. This requirement can be seen from the religious laws generally implemented in some Islamic countries, exerting a far-reaching negative impact on the country and society as a whole.

4. How should the composition of the society with the integration of politics and religion be defined?

Then, how to define the composition of the society with the integration of politics and religion? Such societies are more likely to be formed spontaneously without registration. According to the national law, more than two people breaching the law are regarded as gangs. Thus, by the same token, if more than two people make demands on the public with religious teachings, then I think it can be regarded as an actual society with integration of politics and religion, and when its number becomes increasingly numerous and its power becomes more powerful, it will have a greater negative impact on the public and society.

As for those societies with the integration of politics and religion actually registered, I think its negative impact is not lower than the unregistered societies with the integration of politics and religion, and to a certain extent, it plays a supporting role for those unregistered societies with the integration of politics and religion.

5. Conclusion

Therefore, I deem that any country should be aware of and be vigilant about the integration of politics and religion, rather than ignoring and tolerating it, because any country should only take its own laws as its sole authority, instead of tolerating the existence of such societies with the integration of politics and religion that make demands on society based on religious teachings.

Chapter 7 On the Religious Bundling in

Some Nations

The issue of religious bundling in some nations mentioned in this chapter takes some phenomena existing in Islam as an example. However, in addition to such phenomena existing in Islam today, in some other religions and local cultures in the world, there are also such ethnic and religious cultural bundling phenomena more or less. Thus, since the reason is the same, the same relevant principles also apply here.

1. On the Question of Whether Some Nations Can Eat Pork

In the minds of many people, it seems that there are some Islamic nations in the world who do not eat pork, and the ban on pork already has become a major feature of these nationalities. Therefore, many people will have a question about whether the people of these nations can eat pork.

According to the relevant principles of freedom of faith, this question can actually be said to be a pseudo-proposition. Because according to the basic principle of "separation of nationality and religion" in modern society, since the ban on pork is in accordance with the provisions of Islamic doctrine, and it is also widely implemented among many followers of Islam, it shows that the ban on pork belongs to the category of religion rather than nationality, and has nothing to do with whether the people of these nationalities can eat pork.

In other words, as any nation, whether its people can eat pork should not be a problem in itself, because among the civil rights of a country, everyone has the right to eat pork, and as long as it is not prohibited by national law, everyone can choose to do it on their own. People of any nationality should have their personal freedom right to eat pork, and no one or any nation has the right to interfere with it.

Therefore, with regard to this issue, we can say that if any one of these nations do not believe in Islam, they should not be influenced by Islam and absolutely have the freedom to eat pork. No one has the right to interfere with it. Moreover, if any one of these nations believes in Islam but eats pork, we can only say that he believes in Islam but violates the doctrine, or he is not pious enough to Islam at the most. But his behavior of eating pork belongs to his personal will, and it still falls into the category of individual's freedom, and the basic rights of citizens of a country should naturally be protected by national laws. No one or nation has the right to interfere with it.

To sum up, it can be seen that whether the people of these nations can eat pork should not be a problem, and even those who have already believed in Islam cannot be regarded as a problem, because those who believe in Islam can only be said to be impious even if they eat pork, but their right to eat pork is still protected by national laws, and no one or any nation has the right to interfere with it. As a result, religious believers have no right to have negative opinions and interfere with them.

Finally, I would like to emphasize that the principle of individual freedom of such citizens applies to all peoples and countries in the world that generally believe in Islam, as well as to any place in the world where ethnic and religious bundling is involved.

2. On the Religious Bundling in Some Nations

From a worldwide point of view, religious bundling does exist among some nations who believe in Islam today, but we know that in modern society, the separation of nation and religion is a basic principle. Next, we will discuss the phenomenon of ethnic and religious bundling and how to deal with it correctly.

1.   The difference between these nations and others lies in their religious faiths

First of all, we know that the biggest difference between these nations and others in the world is that these nations have the characteristics of believing in Islam as a whole. When people mention the names of these ethnic groups, it is natural to associate these nations with Islam. Thus, what kind of influence does Islam have on these nations, which makes them different from other nations?

2.   Some problems of forced faith in Islam today

For this, we can first take a look at some of the problems of forced faith practices that exist in Islam in the world, which are mainly characterized by the following two characteristics:

The first is the integration of politics and religion, which mainly exists in some Islamic countries in the Middle East. In these countries, Islamic laws and national laws are always confused. A government and relevant religious communities can demand and even conduct Islamic trials on their citizens in accordance with Islamic laws so that the whole country is affected by the generally applied Islamic laws. It can be seen that some Islamic countries in the Middle East actually feature the integration of politics and religion.

In addition, in some countries with a large proportion of Islamists in the world, Islamic societies can have the right to apply Islamic law to their citizens (especially the Islamists among them) and exert doctrinal demands and influence on the outside world. In fact, some of these countries feature the semi-integration of politics and religion.

The second is the characteristics of ethnic and religious bundling, implemented in some ethnic groups in the world. Among these ethnic groups who believe in Islam, they require that the ethnic groups generally embrace it in the name of the nation, and their people are also characterized by mutual doctrines, labeled with Islam once they were born and are required not to convert their religion for life. To a certain degree, this kind of ethnic and religious binding has led to the loss of the individual right of free choice in religious belief, which actually has a restraining effect on their national freedom.

We can see from the above that the ethnic and religious bundling we discussed here belongs to the second forced belief practice mentioned above, that is, these ethnic groups have the characteristics of ethnic and religious bundling, but not the characteristics of a free nation.

3.   What are the characteristics of a free nation?

Thus, what are the characteristics of a free nation? A basic feature of a free nation is the freedom of faith. That is to say, for any religion, every people can freely choose to believe it or not, and praise it or belittle it. However, at present, under the requirements of the bundling of nationalities and religions that exists in Islam, their people have lost these rights of free belief that originally belong to individuals to a certain extent, which makes its nation seem not to have the characteristics of a free nation.

4.   Status quo of these nations

Such phenomenon exists not only in some Islamic countries, but also in nations in secular countries. In nations bound to religion in today's secular countries, if their people no longer believe in Islam (i.e., withdrawal or conversion), they may not dare to admit it publicly for fear of being pressured by others. On the other hand, if women want to choose a spouse who does not believe in Islam in marriage, they are also likely to be discriminated and offended locally. All these phenomena can be seen as the betrayal of the principle of individual religious belief, that is, it has violated the most fundamental principle of freedom in belief, which is the current situation that the ethnic and religious bundles encountered by the people of these ethnic groups.

5.   Islam does not belong to the free culture of these peoples

To confront the ethnic and religious bindings encountered by these ethnic groups, it is actually incorrect to say that Islam is the culture of these ethnic groups. As fairly speaking, if the implementation of a certain religious doctrine is accompanied by the practice of forced belief, then it is actually a kind of restraint on these bound peoples, rather than a free culture of their nations.

Otherwise, it is unacceptable for a religion to impose its teachings on these people through forced belief practices by claiming that these religious teachings are their national culture. Correctly speaking, some of these religious teachings under the practice of forced belief should not be regarded as their culture. Instead, they can be shackles on their nation. Therefore, only if the Islam would transform into a religion that allows individuals to choose freely, could it be reasonably deemed as their own national and cultural characteristics.

6.   How to help these nations?

Given with the ethnic and religious binding problems of these nationalities today, how can the world really care about and help them? From the above, it can be seen that if we concern about these nations, we must support the granting of freedom, we should take their people's right to freedom of belief into account, and we should oppose the forced belief practices that exist in Islam today, so that each member of these nations can have the individual right to freely choose to believe or not, praise or belittle any religion. Therefore, if we want to care about these nations and their people, we should correctly understand some of the problems of forced belief practices that are common in Islam today, so as to urge them to reform and get rid of the relevant forced belief practices, so as to carry out ethnic and religious separation, in order to restore these nations with free national characteristics, and the individual right to freedom of belief of each of them.

7.   Who are imprisoning the people of these nations today

As for those who demand these peoples with the teachings of Islam and those who generally believe in and abide by their teachings, these people not only cannot be regarded as loving these peoples, but to impose demands on the people of these ethnic groups with religious teachings, it is a manifestation of imprisoning their national freedom. So correctly speaking, some of these people love the forced belief practices that exist in Islam today, rather than giving freedom to every one of them, and they are not those who love these peoples, but those who impose forced beliefs. People who imprison nations are actually people who hurt the freedom of these peoples.

8.   The relevant Islamic societies have the obligation to support the individual right to freedom of belief of the people of these nationalities

In addition, it should be mentioned in particular that in the relevant laws of secular countries, freedom of belief has long been defined. That is, any citizen is free to choose to believe in or not to believe in any religion, as well as the related right to freedom of religious expression.

Therefore, in all secular countries, I think the relevant Islamic societies have the obligation to support the individual freedom of belief of these ethnic groups, rather than imprison the individual freedom of belief of these ethnic groups. Otherwise, it is not to respect their people, but to harm the freedom of belief of their people.

This is just like the Christian and Buddhist associations in China, which do not have the right to require Han, Miao and other nations to believe in only one religion, and it is the same reason that they also have the obligation to support that every nation has the right to freedom of religion. Otherwise, it is engaging in ethnic and religious bundling and the integration of politics and religion, which is contrary to the relevant national laws on freedom of belief.

In addition, in some Islamic countries, since the implementation of religious laws is a common fact, if we want the local Islamic communities in these countries also support the individual right to freedom of belief of these nations, which is, at present, naturally much more difficult, but the same principle applies here.

9.   The need to face this religious binding

To sum up, the main problem faced by these nations today is the problem of religious binding in their own nationalities. In fact, this problem has always been difficult for these ethnic groups to really integrate into the secular society. It is also one of the main reasons why they are different from other ethnic groups.

Thus, I believe that those who really care about their own nation should review the problem of religious binding in their own nations, and should not choose to ignore. Otherwise, it will bring an obstacle in their national development.

10.   The urgency to carry out reform for Islam

In the face of these forced belief practices that exist in Islam today and the actual implementation in some parts of the world, I think it is everyone's responsibility to urge its reform, that is, to transform today's Islam into a separation of politics and religion, or nationality and religion, which can bring everyone the freedom to choose to believe or not, to praise or belittle a normal religious belief. By this approach, the problem of religious binding in those nations in our world that are bound by religion can also be resolved naturally.

Chapter 8 Explaining Religious Beliefs

This chapter draws on explanations of some of the nominal concepts of religious belief in order to illustrate the relevant public cultural nature of religious belief and, in so doing, to illustrate some of the relevant rules of freedom of belief.

1. What Are Religion, Faith, Superstition And Their Differences

It is commonly seen that someone claims himself or herself a person of faith, meaning that he or she has accepted a religious belief. Thus, if we dig deeper, we must ask whether you have accepted a religion, a belief or just a superstition. Before answering this question, we must first clarify the concept of religion, belief and superstition and the difference between them, in order to clarify which of these three you accept.

1. What is religion:

Religion is composed of doctrine and related rituals, and is a doctrinal demand on the person, which has two main effects on the believer, one being a moral constraint on his or her conscience, the other being a religious doctrine or ritual that he or she is required to observe personally, which is equivalent to a form of coercion. It can be seen that religion has two main effects on the believers, that the former, moral constraint, is positive and the latter, coercion, is positive depending on the specific nature of the religion.

2. What is faith:

Faith is a kind of truth-seeking, which not only has the moral constraints of the former, but also has a demand for truth. The nature of faith shall only have positive significance. As for those that are under the name of faith but depart from the nature of faith, that is, truth-seeking, they are not faith.

3. What is superstition:

Superstition is the belief in and fascination with the relevant doctrine, which may initially appear to be a religion. But since it does not allow others to question it or to debate it, it makes the belief a mere fascination, a blind acceptance of what is wrong, and in general, superstition is not beneficial to people.

4.   What is religious belief:

We usually say religious beliefs habitually, that is, we confuse religion and faith. It means that you accept a religion or a faith, but no specific distinction is given, which is a general expression and a statement.

5.   Distinction and relationship between religion and faith:

Religion consists of both doctrine and related rituals, that is, a temporary guardianship or coercion to man, while faith is truth-seeking, which guides man to freedom and truth. Religion is a temporary trusteeship, as in the child stage, while faith is a permanent pursuit and belongs to the adult stage. Religion is between superstition and faith, and is also a transitive dependence. If a religion does not allow people to question, it will fall into a superstition, while religion, if it does, may rise into a faith. This shows that faith is above religion.

Furthermore, religion is a doctrine, a doctrine with a system, a soil for bringing in faith; and faith is a pursuit for truth. Religion itself must ultimately be consistent with faith and truth, and be able to guide people to the pursuit of faith and truth. Otherwise, religion, as a systematic doctrine, can become a shield and a hindrance to people's pursuit of faith and truth, as is the case with much idolatry in the world, which leads to indulgence in it.

6.   The distinction between superstition and faith:

Superstition is when a person believes in one thing and does not allow others to question it. Faith, on the other hand, is when a person believes in the same thing but allows others to question it. Superstition is just a fascination, while faith is a pursuit for truth. Superstition enslaves, while faith makes people independent. Superstition makes people narrow-minded, while faith makes people broad-minded. Superstition tends to create hatred for dissenters, while faith makes people loving.

7.   The distinction between questioning and doubting:

In the light of the explanation above, one may ask, if a person believes that he has accepted a faith, should he not always be skeptical about what he believes in order to show that he has accepted faith but not superstition? The answer, of course, is NO. We need to clarify the difference between questioning and doubting in order to show what the proper attitude to faith should be.

First, a person who truly has an attitude of faith must be one who possesses the ability to question everything and has a keen sense of what is wrong in order to be truth-seeking, but questioning is not the same as doubting, and one does not need to doubt what one believes.

In other words, believing is opposed to doubt, and it is normal for a person to believe in a religious belief without doubting it, but he or she must allow others to question or even doubt his or her religious belief, and if he or she finds that others are justified in questioning it, he or she should also allow himself or herself to question or even doubt the belief in order to seek the truth.

8. Conclusion:

In summary, religion is the soil and dependence of a transition towards faith. When a person begins to accept a religious belief, it is more like the beginning of personally accepting a religion in terms of experience. But slowly this religious faith must guide him or her to move towards faith, towards truth-seeking, and to believe while allowing others and himself or herself to question (and to question if errors are found), and this is true faith. But if other's questioning or debating is not allowed, then it is more in the realm of superstition.

In this regard, everyone can also refer to the above mentioned distinction between religion, faith and superstition to identify whether they are believing a religion, faith or superstition.

2. Explanation of Several Religious Terms And Related Boundaries of Freedom of Faith

We know that today there are different religions in the world, and within the same religion there are many different religious groups (or organizations, the same below), and these different religious groups are separated from each other by their own understanding of doctrine and religious practices, and therefore, in order to show that they are more authentic, there are some mutual criticisms and even derogatory practices among each other.

According to my observation, some criticisms and derogatory terms used by these different religious groups often mislead people who do not understand the concept of religion, and such misunderstanding may affect the public's understanding of the freedom of belief. Therefore, in the following, I will explain and clarify several terms that are easily misunderstood, and in this way, illustrate the boundaries of the freedom of belief.

1.   The difference between religious fanaticism and religious extremism:

At present, many people often get confused between religious fanaticism and religious extremism, mistakenly believing that both are abnormal religious practices and dismissing them as such. In fact, however, the two are not identical in nature and are two different concepts that should be specifically distinguished.

(1) What is religious fanaticism:

By religious fanaticism, it means that when a person has adopted a religion, it is easily seen by outsiders as a religious fanaticism or even unwise behavior because of personal devotion and zeal, such as being willing to sacrifice one's time and energy, or willing to give one's precious possessions to devote, etc. But in any case, this so-called religious devotion or religious fanaticism is, rightly or wrongly, a personal and free pursuit, that is, it is a normal practice of personal religious faith that demands doctrine of oneself and not of others.

(2) What is religious extremism:

Religious extremism is when a person has adopted a religion, he or she not only requires himself or herself by religious doctrine, but also resorts to violence to require and force others by religious doctrine, thereby resulting in a certain degree of illegality, which naturally is not a normal practice of religious belief.

(3) Public distinctions between the two:

From the above, it is clear that, in terms of the public nature of society, so-called religious fanaticism is actually a normal behavior of personal religious belief, which is in line with the principle of freedom of belief. In contrast, religious extremism involves specific violent acts of doctrinal demands and coercion against others, in violation of the relevant principle of freedom of belief.

2. Distinction between heresies and cults:

It is the customary understanding of many people today that "heresy" and "cult" are the same thing, that they are both equally negative terms, and easily to be confused from each other. Because of this, they are usually referred to collectively as Because of this, they are often referred to collectively as "heretic cult" and given the same negative treatment. In fact, however, heresy and cult are not identical in nature, but belong to two different concepts, which should be specifically distinguished.

(1) What is heresy:

Heresy refers to the perception and identification of a religious group (or groups) of the same religion with a particular religious group. It is generally based on the perception that a religious group is different from one's own in its religious practices and, in particular, that the other group is unconventional and deviates from the orthodox principles of the religion in its understanding and application of a particular religious doctrine, and therefore derogatorily calls the other group a heresy.

It follows that the term "heresy" is a perception and identification of one or more religious groups on another between different religious groups, and that such identification does not have socially public properties. In other words, while the term "heresy" may be pejorative for different religious groups within the same religion, it is neutral from a socially public point of view, and the so-called "heretic" religious groups are still normal religious groups in accordance with the law of the country.

Let me illustrate this with an example. For example, in the Christian Bible, in the early stages of Christianity, it was opposed by the Jews as a heresy because it differed from traditional Jewish practices, but it was not actually illegal under the laws of the time. In other words, what was considered heresy in the eyes of the Jews at the time was not illegal in the eyes of the society at the time, but the term "heresy" was a neutral term.

(2) What is cult:

In brief, a cult is a religion that may be recognized as such when the doctrinal claims of the religion, and the actual implementation of those doctrines, have been involved in breaking the law of the country, such as hurting and killing people.

(3) Public distinctions between heresies and cults:

As can be seen from above, the relevant religious acts referred to by the term "heresy" are not illegal from the point of view of social public properties and national law, and are neutral terms that belong to normal religious beliefs. Cult refers to a religious group whose doctrinal implementation is characterized by violent practices that are contrary to the law and is a negative term, not belong to normal religious beliefs.

Chapter 9 On Nationalities,

Multiculturalism and Universal Harmony

This chapter draws on the relevant explanations of nationalities, multiculturalism and universal harmony to illustrate that the ultimate goal and outcome of freedom of belief is to move towards a world of universal harmony. One of the main features of a world of universal harmony is the universal possession of the right rules of freedom of belief on the planet and the consequent absence of a soil for forced beliefs.

1. Is nationalism wrong?

It is common to see many netizens who oppose nationalism, and there are many who put down those who care about their own nation as a narrow act that creates a divide between peoples and seems to go against the universal value of equality of nations, so is nationalism wrong in modern society?

1.　The difference between nationalism and ultra-nationalism:

Here we should first clarify and distinguish between "nationalism" and "ultra-nationalism" to avoid confusion, if, according to the relevant sources, in brief.

Nationalist refers to a person who cares for the interest of his or her own nation, works and serves in the interests of his or her own people, especially when the interests of his or her own people are harmed.

Ultra-nationalist refers to a person that satisfies and expands the interests of his or her own nation at the expense of the interests of other nations, including by the means of exploitation, oppression and aggression of other nations.

It is clear from the foregoing that ultra-nationalism is naturally undesirable, but that proper nationalism means caring for and protecting the interests of one's own people, especially when they are harmed. Such values should then be acceptable to all.

2.　Order of external concern of each person:

Here, the author will explain something about the order of external concern of each person living in this world, in order to have a clearer illustration of the above points. The order of concern should be like this: 1. for oneself and one's family; 2. for one's friends and neighbors; 3. for one's fellow-countrymen; and 4. for all people in the world. It is narrow if one thinks that one needs to care only for the former and therefore deny the latter, but hollow if one thinks that one shall care for the latter but not the former.

In this order, we see that if nationalism is based on blood and regional identity, the order shall be love for one's own family, love for one's own fellow countrymen, and it shall be based on justice and on a empathy of the suffering of other nations and countries, then this nationalism must be well-received. But if it is ultra-nationalism, such as the expansion of one's own interests at the expense of the interests of others, then that is what should be opposed.

3.   Whether nationalism is contrary to racial equality:

In this regard, there is also the concern that if nationalism is contrary to racial equality, and of course it is not. For racial equality means that there must be no racial discrimination, and love for one's fellow countrymen is not the same as discrimination against others. This is just as absurd as it would be for someone to think that loving family and friends and fellow countrymen is discrimination against others.

Thus, nationalism and racial equality are two concepts that do not contradict each other.

4.   Does nationalism bring in division:

Another concern is whether nationalism will bring in inter-ethnic divisions and divide the country. Certainly not! It is as if one loves one's family and friends, does that create national divisions? Certainly not! For the same reason, normal love for the people of the same nation and country does not produce national or world division.

Also, ultra-nationalism is different from nationalism to make this possible, but that's a different subject.

5.   What are the goals of nationalism:

The goal of nationalism is to achieve the normal civil rights of the people of one's own nation in a country. By republicanism, we mean that all nations have the same normal civil rights in a country, and that if all nations in a country have the same civil rights, they will naturally be brought into a state of integration.

6.   Conclusion:

In the light of the foregoing, it is essential to understand and clarify what nationalism is, because to deny nationalism is in fact the same as denying the private domain of love for one's family and friends and neighbors. Therefore, the right attitude is to understand everything just right, but not over, otherwise, denying the right nationalism is as incorrect as supporting ultra-nationalism, which are incorrect perspectives.

2. What is Multiculturalism?

Many people have the impression that multiculturalism means the coexistence of various cultures in a society. However, there is a problem with this: as cultures have their strengths and shortcomings, there is naturally a competition among cultures. Some cultures may be harmful to society, so it is difficult for cultures to coexist. What does true multiculturalism look like? This article will discuss and clarify this.

1.   Definition of multiculturalism

First of all, we have to ask: by respecting for multiculturalism, does it mean respecting for people or respect for culture? The answer, of course, is that it means respect for people. Culture itself, which has both good sides and bad sides, can be praised or criticized, and does not need to be respected for.

It follows that the respect for multiculturalism means respecting the right of each individual to make a diverse and autonomous choice of cultures, so that society can be selective for multiple cultures, giving prominence to the richness and diversity of the society.

But unlike the above, respect for multiculturalism does not in any way mean that the coexistence of cultures should be protected and that the competition between different cultures should therefore be restricted, thus forcing the population to accept the coexistence of all cultures.

The above comparison shows that respect for people and respect for culture are to some extent contradictory; respect for people is respect for multiculturalism, while respect for culture may end up anti-multiculturalism.

2.   What cultures are multi-culture?

It is clear from the above that for a culture to be multi-culture, it must, first of all, offer people the right to choose, that is, the right to choose freely whether to praise it or not, and whether to accept it or not. This culture must then have the following two conditions.

(1) Not contrary to national law.

For example, the corrupt culture of female circumcision is not part of multiculturalism because it is directly contrary to the law of the country. Another example is the Chinese practice of female foot-binding, which is also clearly against the law of the country because it causes physical disabilities to women, and is clearly not part of multiculturalism.

(2) No coerciveness contained.

For example, there are religious cultures that contain coercive beliefs and other cultures that contain coerciveness. Since they are coercive, they violate the principle of the survival of the fittest and are inherently anti-multicultural and are clearly not part of multiculturalism.

3.   Which cultures can the country promote?

In the context of multicultural competition, it is the right of a country or nation to advocate for some cultures, especially the dominant culture of the country and nation, as a privilege of predominance. However, this right is only the right to advocate, not to compel, and does not interfere with or affect the right of the population to make its own personal choice of diverse cultures.

In addition, the country may provide appropriate protection for distinctive cultures that may fade away with the course of history, but such protection remains limited to a form of advocacy and does not interfere with and force the population to accept such cultures, but rather respects their right to personal and autonomous choice.

4.   What cultures are aggressive cultures?

In a multicultural society, some areas that originally had only a relatively inferior culture may experience a greater impact from the superior foreign culture and some of the local cultures may even be changed, so are some of these foreign cultures considered a form of cultural aggression?

Of course not, and here we must recognize what an aggressive culture is.

Any culture, whether local or foreign, is a part of multiculturalism and not an aggressive culture, as long as it allows the population to choose on its own and have the right to praise or criticize it freely, and competes with other cultures.

However, if a culture is inherently coercive and does not offer the population the right to choose and to praise or criticize it freely, and that does not allow competition with other cultures, it is of the nature of cultural aggression and not part of multiculturalism.

5. The significance of multiculturalism

In a multicultural society, as a result of the competition among cultures, the cultures themselves will naturally undergo a certain degree of process of selecting the essence and discarding the gross, and become a relatively harmless or even beneficial culture with its own characteristics. When such cultures gather together in a society, the richness and diversity of the society is given prominence to, being the value and significance of multiculturalism.

6. The role of multiculturalism

Here, we would discuss the positive effects of multiculturalism on a country and a nation, which are reflected in three aspects as follows.

(1) Promoting social integration:

In a multicultural society, as each person has the right to make his or her own choice of cultures and the right to freely choose to praise or criticize them, and as a result everyone respects each other and tolerate the differences, a common perception of multiculturalism is created, which naturally leads to a state of social integration, that is, republicanism.

We can hereby clarify one concept. In the past, it was often said that national identity was a cultural identity. But now it seems that we can more accurately say that national identity is based on identification with the correct multiculturalism of the country.

For example, although there are many different local cultures and various religious cultures in a country, these different cultures do not divide the society, but rather, under the competition of multiple cultures, the superior survives and the inferior is eliminated. To a certain extent, each culture takes the best of other cultures and discards the worst of its own, promoting a kind of integration and progress of the society.

In addition, it is only those cultures that are themselves contrary to the law of the country and those with a compulsive nature, which are not belong to multicultural, would divide the society, other than integrating it.

(2) Promoting cultural enhancement

As mentioned earlier, in a multicultural society, all cultures go through a process of taking the best and discarding the worst to a certain extent, and can become a relatively harmless or even beneficial culture with its own characteristics.

It is evident then that the right kind of multiculturalism can only bring some kind of improvement, but not decline, to a region's culture. For areas that are less developed culturally, they even have the blessing of recreating culture.

(3) Promoting moral advancement

Here, we are going to discuss the moral impact of cultural advancement on a region.

First of all, we have to distinguish that morality is divided into public and private moralities. Institutional rules mainly influence the public morality of the population, while culture mainly influences the private morality of the population.

For example, in parts of the world where institutional rules are better, the population is relatively better in public morals, while in parts of the world where the culture is better, the population is relatively better in private morals. Meanwhile, a better culture will also naturally advance the local social system. It should also be noted that the word "relatively" is used here, not "absolutely", as otherwise it might involve geographical or ethnic discrimination.

Therefore, in a multicultural society, as the culture of a region advances, it will inevitably have a positive impact on the private morality of the local population and even advance the local social system, that is, public morality that promotes positive impact. In other words, multiculturalism will promote the overall cultural and moral level of a region.

7. Conclusion

To sum up, multiculturalism means respecting the right of each individual to make his or her own choice of culture, rather than protecting the simultaneous existence of various cultures. In a multicultural society, through the competition among cultures, all cultures will undergo a certain degree of taking the best and discarding the worst, and will all become relatively harmless or even beneficial cultures with their own characteristics. And when such cultures gather together in a society, they reveal the richness and diversity of the society and improve the social integration and the overall cultural morality of a region.

3. Differences in the Nature of Several Related Terms, Such As Cosmopolitanism and Universal Harmony

Many people think that the terms cosmopolitanism, globalism, internationalism, universal harmony, globalization and global village are the same thing, but they are wrong. There are opposite meanings of these terms, even in terms of values, and many people get confused.

To classify these terms, cosmopolitanism, globalism and internationalism are in the same group, and universal harmony, globalization and global village are in the same group. These are two groups of words with completely different meanings, of which difference I will explain below.

You should have seen the obvious difference in these words. The first group has the word "ism" in it, while the second group does not have it, and therein lies the difference.

And what does "ism" mean? It means a proposition, that is, the former group is a proposition, while the latter group does not have an proposition; the latter group is, in fact, an adjective.

Let's start with the first group.

First of all, globalism and cosmopolitanism, global means world. Furthermore, the word "international" in internationalism also means the concept regardless of national boundaries, i.e., the world, so all three terms have the meaning of cosmopolitanism, and they all mean roughly the same thing.

And what do these three words mean? It means that there should be no distinction between nations in this world, and that it should be advocated that there are no national boundaries or ethnic distinctions, but only world citizenship. In other words, it means that it is necessary to establish a practice of absolute mutual disinterest among different nations.

Then some people may ask, isn't absolute selflessness a good thing? But in fact, heaven is hell. Absolute selflessness means that without boundaries, there will bring about a chaos of rules. In reality, countries with such an approach will actually produce various reverse elimination effects, such as the production of various reverse nationalism practices.

Then why is that so? It is because it is legitimate for countries to seek their own interests, and it is normal for each country to seek the interests of itself and its own people, and this is not inconsistent with mutual assistance and contact, because no country should sell its own national interests for mutual assistance and contact.

Thus, where this set of words goes wrong is in negating the aspect of seeking legitimate interests for one's own country. It is actually quite legitimate for a country or nation to fight for the interests of its own countrymen under the relevant international legal rules. It is just as legitimate for a family to fight for the interests of its own families under the rules of law. Both family and nation are in the same way.

At this point, someone might ask, is it wrong to be a "internationalist" to help others? To answer this question, we must recognize the difference between the public and private approaches.

On the individual level, it is true that a person can give his or her utmost or even selfless help to an unrelated person in a distant place crossing the concepts of family, nation and country, and such help is indeed a manifestation of selfless great-love because it crosses the boundaries of family, friends and nation. However, such great-love should be limited to the practice of giving to individuals only and not to the practice of giving at the national public level.

For if a country's public policy practice is to go to great lengths to help other countries crossing its own citizens, or to disregard its own civil interests, even at the expense of its own national interests, this, on the contrary, appears to be abnormal, and is actually a practice betraying its own public interests.

Thus, if it is the "internationalism" of individuals, it would be more accurate, in my view, to use the term "international great-love" instead of "internationalism", in accordance with the facts. Because it does not involve the public issue between nations. And if it is normal mutual assistance between countries, it should only be called "international assistance", but not "internationalism", because, in the final analysis, "internationalism" is, in terms of the public level, a term that has certain ideological requirements.

Then let's talk about the second group.

In the terms that globalization, global village, and universal harmony, there is no "ism" in them. Thus, there is no proposition or claim, which proves that these terms are actually adjectives or descriptions of a certain situation in the world.

First of all, what is universal harmony? It means that the countries of the world are roughly the same, yet different in some way. Thus, its difference from the first group above is that universal harmony does not seek to make the world the same. Universal harmony and cosmopolitanism (the pursuit of sameness) are two different things.

And what is the vision of universal harmony? It means that all the countries of the world are well, that everyone lives and works in peace and prosperity. There might be borders, but they are friendly with each other. This is like the families of a village, where everyone can interact well and be at peace with each other, but it does not mean that this peace can eliminate families, that there is no need for the concept of family. On the contrary, the elimination of the concept of family is a cosmopolitan approach.

Here, we are comparing the countries of the world with the families of a village, and we should have understood that this is what is meant by a global village. Moreover, globalization also means better communication among countries, such as better information transmission. Therefore, it also means global village. Therefore, universal harmony, globalization and global village all roughly mean the same thing.

Now, since the two groups of words mentioned represent two different meanings, the author will only use the words "cosmopolitanism" and "universal harmony" to illustrate these two different pursuits in the world nowadays, so as to better explain the different meanings and distinctions between these two groups of words.

Then what is cosmopolitanism? Cosmopolitanism is essentially the idea that the nations of the world should cede all or part of their sovereign interests and form a single world-like country.

And what is universal harmony? It is a world in which all nations are at peace, where each has its own national sovereignty and borders, but they live in harmony and friendship with each other.

Thus, in terms of the public level of relations between countries, cosmopolitanism is a claim that requires countries to cede their sovereignty and related interests, while universal harmony is a phenomenon in which countries fight for their interests, assist and interact with each other under relevant international rules. One is a demand (a public proposition means a claim with a public demand) and the other is a phenomenon, and that is the fundamental difference in the nature of the two groups of terms.

4. What Does Universal Harmony Look Like?

Universal harmony is what human beings pursue and long for all along. However, many people have misunderstandings about what universal harmony is, thinking that it is a homogeneous world in which all nations and peoples are identical. But in fact, this is not the case. Nowadays, with the development process of modern social civilization, we can get the help to start to have some clearer understanding and expectation of universal harmony.

In general terms, universal harmony must have, first and foremost, the following three essential characteristics.

1.   Countries around the world have a relatively universal state of institutional democratization.

2.   The world will no longer contain a living soil for compulsive religious doctrine and cultures.

3.   On the basis of the two previous points, freedom of individual and autonomous belief prevails among all the peoples of the world.

In other words, on the basis of the above three points, universal harmony is equivalent to a worldwide harmony in which people have relatively universal democracy in their institutions and personal autonomy in their beliefs. Universal harmony does not mean that all nations and peoples are identical and homogeneous, but that all nations and peoples of the world, while having their own distinctive cultures, can have an overall tolerant environment that is harmonious, while tolerate the differences from each other, so that the whole world can be in a prosperous environment in which all things compete but are in harmony with each other. Universal harmony shall be worth pursuing and longing for by all people.

However, there are still many people misunderstand the concept of universal harmony and deem that, since the world's civilization progress will ultimately advance towards universal harmony, the nations of the world should promote cosmopolitanism. In other words, it is advocated that a country should strive only for the interests of the world and not focus only on its own particular national interests, and thus negates the notion that a country must strive for the interests of its own citizens and peoples, which is, of course, awfully wrong.

Universal harmony means more freely traveling among the nations of the world for individuals, and, to a certain extent, dilute national boundaries, but it does not mean that a country should not strive for the interests of its own country, its own people and nation. On the contrary, as long as such striving is carried out in accordance with the relevant international rules and does not take the form of aggression against other nations and peoples, it is legitimate and does not deviate from the idea of republicanism or even universal harmony.

We can illustrate this more clearly by simply taking the example of the republic of a nation. This multicultural and republican harmony of the world is like a country with many different nationalities, families and even a large number of citizens, all of whom may be different or even in competition with each other, but can nevertheless be republican and even mutually supportive, as is the case with universal harmony.

It is clear from the foregoing that in universal harmony, although each country and nation is different from the other, they are in harmony with each other, showing the richness and variety of the world. Although they compete with each other in the rules, they do not infringe upon each other, showing the characteristics of republic and even mutual assistance.

www.ingramcontent.com/pod-product-compliance
Lightning Source LLC
Chambersburg PA
CBHW020419130626
46549CB00006B/2638